THE CATHOLIC VIEWPOINT SERIES

Editor: John J. Delaney

CATHOLIC VIEWPOINT

ON CHURCH AND STATE

Jerome G. Kerwin

Professor of Political Science
University of Chicago

HANOVER HOUSE
A DIVISION OF DOUBLEDAY & COMPANY, INC.

Garden City, New York
1960

Nihil Obstat: James A. Reynolds, Ph.D.
          Censor Librorum

Imprimatur: ✠ Francis Cardinal Spellman
          Archbishop of New York
          May 10, 1960

The nihil obstat *and imprimatur are official declarations
that a book or pamphlet is free of doctrinal or moral error.
No implication is contained therein that those who have
granted the nihil obstat and imprimatur agree with the
contents, opinions, or statements expressed.*

Contents

1117726

Contents

Introduction

During the past few decades the position and attitude of the Catholic Church in the United States on a variety of subjects has been more and more closely scrutinized. Her unceasing labors in alleviating human want and misery in the form of hospitals, orphanages, foundling homes have attracted universal approbation; the uncompromising position she has taken in certain areas where she has felt her basic teachings were threatened has frequently aroused opposition and sometimes open hostility. Censorship, divorce, birth control, education are some of the areas of human activity in which her stand has been questioned and opposed.

In the final analysis, these areas of disagreement are but segments of an all-encompassing problem which should be studied to place these subsidiary problems in their proper perspective. This problem is simply: What is the role of the Church in the modern American democracy, and specifically what is the position of the Catholic Church in our society? A reasonable answer to these questions is desirable, and even essential, if a rational consideration of the component problem areas is to be of any value.

The problem of the relationship between Church and state has occupied men's minds for centuries. With the dawn of the Christian era, the emphasis of Christianity on the dignity and worth of the individual, and on the primary allegiance of man to God rather than to any human agency, immediately posed the problem of the relationship of man's supernatural allegiance and his functions and duties in a man-made society. Granted that man's ultimate and all-encompassing goal is to attain heaven, it is still a fact he has a life to live on earth in association with other men—a fact which requires a government administered by men.

Men early posed the Church's problem when the chief priests and scribes attempted to trap Christ into a treasonable statement. His reply, "Render therefore to Caesar the things that are Caesar's, and to God the things that are God's" was a God-given statement for all Christians that there were to be two societies on earth and each was entitled to man's allegiance and support. Having once stated the principle, He left it to man to evolve the institutions necessary to make this basic tenet effective.

And through the centuries men have wrestled with this problem. The theories governing the relationship between Church and state have ranged from complete ecclesiastical control of the officers of the state to a concept which considers the Church as a branch of the state. The first is typified by St. Ambrose's blunt statement that "the emperor is within the Church, not above the Church" and Pope Gelasius I's letter to Emperor Anastasius I in which he spelled out in unequivocal terms the supremacy of the spiritual authority: "There are indeed, Most August Emperor, two powers by which this world is chiefly ruled: the sacred authority of the popes and the royal power. Of these the priestly power is much more important, because it has to render account for the kings of men themselves at the divine tribunal. For you know, our very clement son, that although you have the chief place in dignity over the human race, yet you must submit yourself faithfully to those who have charge of divine things, and look to them for the means of your salvation." The other extreme runs the gamut from the claim of the Roman emperors that all power was theirs to the modern theory of such rulers as Henry VIII of England and Joseph II of Austria, who acknowledged ecclesiastical authority but merely as an arm of the all-supreme state, as represented by their persons. This latter claim achieved its ultimate goal in the fanatical dictatorship of Adolf Hitler and the present ruling clique in Russia—both dedicated to the aggrandizement of the state and the ruthless extermination of any belief in God as a threat to the total power of the state.

Most men in Western civilization have taken a position between these two extremes but have consistently believed that where a government imposes demands on its citizens in direct conflict with their spiritual beliefs, there can be no course but resistance. Throughout history men have repeatedly indicated their willingness to sacrifice their lives for their beliefs. The martyrs of the early Christian era—men like Thomas à Becket and Thomas More—and in the present day men like Martin Nie-möller in Germany, Cardinal Mindszenty of Hungary, and Bishop Walsh in China offer irrefutable testimony of man's unconquerable insistence that no earthly power can take precedence over his spiritual life.

In the United States the ultimate sacrifice for a man's religious beliefs has never been required. From the very founding of the nation Americans have insisted on the right of men to worship according to their conscience. In the framing of the Constitution, the founding fathers repeatedly affirmed their belief in an almighty Being, and carefully safeguarded man's right to worship this Being as he saw fit. It should be noted in passing that at no time did the founding fathers believe in or propose an inseparable wall between the government and God. Their concern was to prevent the establishment of any particular sect as the state religion.

Obviously, of course, the discussions on religion in the Constitutional Convention and the religion clause in the Constitution did not eliminate religious problems in the American society. For once the government acknowledged the existence of a supreme Being, then the problem which remained to be solved was the centuries-old problem of delineating as sharply and clearly as possible the position of the Church in this new society. And this has been and is a continuing, ever-developing relationship. As a matter of fact, as Dr. Kerwin points out in the text of this book, during the colonial period and, indeed, even under the federal government, an established religion was a not unusual feature of colony and state government. Gradually, the provisions of the federal Constitution were adopted in the individual states until in time all religions were disestablished in the states.

Nevertheless, problems did remain and with the growth of Catholicism in the United States some of these problems tended to become aggravated. Frequently, distortion of the Church's true position has caused further misunderstanding. And nowhere has this been so true as in the field of Church-state relations. Claims that the pope is just waiting for a Catholic to be elected President to move into the White House and rule the country and that Catholics are biding their time until they are a majority to impose their religion on America are presented from some sources as sober fact. Absurd? Of course. But absurd though they are, they must be constantly refuted for the unfounded, irresponsible attacks they are. Their proponents in some cases are deliberately promoting bigotry and anti-Catholicism. With such as these we have no concern in the pages of this book. They are the descendants of the Nativist and Know Nothing movement of the nineteenth century and the unfortunately not entirely moribund Ku Klux Klan. But many who have heard these claims, even while dismissing the most lurid of the accusations against the Catholic Church, are genuinely concerned as to whether there is any validity in whole or in part to many of the assertions that have been made about the Church's position and intent.

Many non-Catholic Americans are curious as to why, on the one hand, in a Catholic country like Spain, there seems to be no religious freedom, while on the other hand, Catholics in the United States angrily denounce accusations that they would deprive their fellow Americans of their religious freedom if they overnight became the majority religion in the United States. For their part, Catholics do not understand why their fellow citizens see no incongruity in raising this line of reasoning for Catholics when crippling disabilities are placed on Catholic freedom in several of the Scandinavian countries; also why those raising the specter of Spain never mention Catholic countries such as Ireland, Belgium, and Brazil, to mention a few, which extend religious freedom to non-Catholics. And, of course, they ask why a Catholic President of a Protestant United States would pay any more heed to clerical advice than does a Catholic President De Gaulle of Catholic France, who has never been accused of allowing the Vatican to interfere with his duties as leader of the French people. Most important of all, their explanations that through the centuries the Church has consistently emphasized she can exist in any society that permits her children to practice their religion and that such *modus vivendi* does not constitute an endorsement of any particular form of government usually falls on deaf ears.

The position of the Church in a democracy differs from her position under other forms of government. The Church existed and endured under such diverse regimes as the Roman Empire, during the feudal eras, and in Bismarck's Germany. Any thinking person must realize that the Church's position varied in each of these societies. By the same token, any consideration of the Catholic Church's position in Spain or in some of the South American countries should not be considered as representative of her attitudes and stands in the United States. These countries possess a different culture, customs, language, and government from ours, and their people often have an entirely different viewpoint on many matters from that held by Americans in the United States.

Catholics in the United States ask merely that their record as American citizens be considered in the light of their participation in the American society, not least of which is the willingness with which they have given up their lives in defense of the United States in every war from the Revolution to the Korean action.

The remarks of two Catholic prelates are so appropriate to these considerations that I ask the reader's forbearance in quoting them, since Dr. Kerwin does quote one of them in the text. I feel the points each stresses is important enough to warrant constant repetition. The first statement was penned in 1901 by Cardinal Gibbons, probably the greatest churchman American Catholicism has produced:

"American Catholics rejoice in our separation of Church and state, and I can conceive no combination of circumstances likely to arise which would make a union desirable for either Church or state."

The second is by Archbishop Egidio Vagnozzi, the highest-ranking representative of the Holy See in the United States:

"As far as the United States is concerned, I feel that it is a true interpretation of the feelings of the Hierarchy and of American Catholics in general to say that they are well satisfied with their Constitution and pleased with the fundamental freedom enjoyed by their Church; in fact, they believe that this freedom is to a large extent responsible for the expansion and consolidation of the Church in this great country.

"Whether they remain a minority or become a majority, I am sure that American Catholics will not jeopardize their cherished religious freedom in exchange for a privileged position."

To which sentiments the overwhelming majority of Catholics in the United States completely and unreservedly subscribe.

It is the purpose of this Catholic Viewpoint volume to offer an explanation of the role of the Catholic Church in the American democracy as envisaged by a leading political scientist who is a Catholic, a distinguished civic leader, and a respected citizen. Once again it is our earnest hope that a frank, straightforward presentation of a complex problem by an authority in the field will help clear up, to some extent, at least, confusion which has helped build up misunderstanding among our fellow citizens.

John J. Delaney

CATHOLIC VIEWPOINT
ON CHURCH AND STATE

The author wishes to acknowledge with deep appreciation the services of Salvatore Ratella as typist, Robert A. Kennedy as proofreader, and Dan Herr, who inspired this work.

CHAPTER I

The Development of a Theory

Christianity introduced a new principle in the relationship between the secular and the spiritual. The world had known theocracies where little distinction existed between the political order and the divine order. It had known in the Greek city state and in Rome the dominance of the political order where religion occupied the position of a department of the state. Christ's teaching that man should "Render unto Caesar the things that are Caesar's and to God the things that are God's" became for Christianity a guiding principle of the new dispensation. Christ's message was largely a spiritual message. He said little about the inequity and the corruption of the Roman rule, but his teachings furnished the standards of judgment by which men could test the justice of any regime. From his teachings, however, Christians did draw the principle of two existing orders, each justified in its own sphere of operation.

During the period of the Roman persecutions Christians might well have questioned, and often did, the legitimacy of the political order. How could a good Christian accept the legitimacy of a political order directed by unbelievers? The kingdoms of the world were judged and condemned. Could justice in any sense be found in a pagan political order, corrupt and licentious, which persecuted the followers of God's law? This constituted the only political order they knew. It was relatively easy for many of the early Christians to condemn the world as they knew it and the political systems that ruled the world. To them there existed only one *order*—the spiritual.

Without question the tendency of many early Christians toward rebellion against the civil authorities caused no little concern among the leaders of the Christians in apostolic terms. Two groups among the Christians may be distinguished according to their attitude toward civil power. Jewish converts to Christianity by inheritance possessed a strong antipathy to Roman rule, and many Gentiles, thoroughly caught up in their new way of life, believed that the only law was God's law and that an anarchic order from the civil point of view was in every way justifiable. The exhortations of both St. Peter and St. Paul on civil obedience were undoubtedly directed toward these groups. To counteract these tendencies, St. Peter admonished his followers: "Be subject to every ordinance of man for the Lord's sake: whether it be to the king, as supreme; or unto governors, as sent by him for vengeance on evil doers and for praise for them that do well"[1] St. Paul in like manner writes in his epistle to the Romans: "Let every soul be in subjection to the higher powers: for there is no power but of God; and the powers that be are ordained of God. Therefore he that resisteth the power withstandeth the ordinance of God; and they that withstand shall receive to themselves judgment."[2]

Even a pagan political power, therefore, could rightfully command obedience, inasmuch as all power stemmed from God. Nor do we find in their teachings any hint of a suggestion that man could live a life of pure anarchy in the civil order. Many converts to Christianity might well have interpreted the freedom of the sons of God as meaning a contempt for all things temporal, including the political order. This attitude no doubt was fortified by the character of the governors under whom the early Christians lived precarious lives.

Specifically, what the early Church asked of the temporal power was freedom to live and to teach. It asked for no special position. The state, however, regarded the Church as an enemy composed of eccentric, troublesome, subversive people who would not give the commonly required reverence and worship due the emperor, and who condemned all prevailing cults as idolatrous.

The conversion of Constantine and the recognition of Christianity as the religion of the Empire brought new problems. A few writers, perhaps out of sheer gratitude, overemphasized the

[1] I Peter, 2:13–17.
[2] Romans, 13:1–7.

power of the state. Ambrosiaster's statement that the king is the vicar of God possessing the image of God and that the bishop has the image of Christ is far more the exceptional than the usual point of view. More commonly, one reads of warnings to the emperor that churchmen do not recognize his authority in spiritual matters. Most writers are emphatic: the emperor has no right to interfere in Church affairs. On the other hand, the churchmen recognize the power of the state in the suppression of heresy and schism. After enumerating the basic doctrines of the Catholic faith we find the Emperor Theodosius in 380 decreeing: "We order those who follow this doctrine to receive the title of Catholic Christians, but others we judge to be mad and raving and worthy of incurring the disgrace of heretical teaching, nor are their assemblies to receive the name of Churches. They are to be punished not only by Divine retribution but also by our own measures, which we have decided in accordance with Divine inspiration."[3] Normally it is accepted that secular penalties could be imposed for spiritual offenses. In other words, the Church judged in spiritual matters; the temporal authority applied the judgment. As a consequence, the temporal power frequently found itself, in moments of intense ecclesiastical strife, not only the executioner of secular penalties, but the judge in ecclesiastical matters.

From St. Ambrose of Milan (340–97), one may draw a more complete theory of temporal and spiritual relations. He points out the necessity of obedience to the civil ruler but at the same time insists that the ruler is a son of the Church and, like all sons of the Church, is subject to Church discipline. The emperor is *in* the Church; he is not set over it. In consequence, he must obey the Church in all things spiritual. Most famous of the practical applications of Ambrose's theory is his exclusion of the Emperor Theodosius from Mass because of the Emperor's responsibility for a massacre in Thessalonica. The Emperor performed the required penance before he was again admitted to the celebration of the Mass.

St. Ambrose takes a very firm position in all of his dealings with the Emperor. He reproves the Emperor for compelling

[3] Theodosiani libri XVI, Vol. I-II, "De Fide Catholica," p. 833.

Christians to rebuild a synagogue which they have burned. He refuses to answer a summons to appear before an imperial court. He bluntly informs the Emperor he will not turn over a church to the Arians even when ordered to do so. He would, however, surrender his private property if the Emperor demanded it. He does seem to draw a distinction on property matters between lands belonging to the Church and church buildings. He is willing under certain circumstances to surrender the former, but never the latter. Throughout his writings and his actions he insists upon the independence of the Church, denying absolute power to the civil ruler, and at the same time protesting respect for the temporal ruler in matters exclusively temporal.

A more complete consideration of the relationship of the temporal to the spiritual is found in the writings of St. Augustine (354-430). He readily accepts the proposition that man must live in association with his fellows; man is a social being. Man, however, is not by nature lord over man. How then explain authority, government, and civil coercion? St. Augustine insists that while civil government exists because of sin, it is nevertheless a *divine remedy* for sin.

The state is not the widest society to which men belong; the widest society is the society of all men under the kingship of God. God's law governs this society and all institutions within it. And God's law is justice. The state is just, in so far as it observes in its actions God's law. St. Augustine does not deny that a state is any less a state if it does not fulfill the commands of the divine law. He tells us that a state is a multitude of men brought together in some bond of agreement. It may therefore be just, partially just, or largely unjust. It does, however, aim at a concord of men in ordered relations with one another. It brings peace. This ordered peace and security which the state affords is good and men render obedience to the civil power. Peace enables the Christian to pursue his spiritual destiny and for this basic reason he obeys civil authority.

But the higher law, the law of God, mediated through the Church, must be obeyed. By it all institutions of men are judged. If the state commands what contradicts this law, the Christian will not obey. The Christian renders obedience to the temporal authority for the salvation of his soul, or if the pursuance of this end becomes impossible by action of the civil authority, the Christian's obligation of obedience ceases. No man owes absolute obedience to the state. Because of God's law he obeys the civil authority but in obedience to the same law he may refuse obedience.

This teaching has been of the utmost importance in the history of Western Europe. It involves a distinction between the secular and the religious spheres. It means that the secular authority is subordinate to a higher law, a higher standard, and that a higher authority judges in the realm of the higher law. The Church or man's conscience must judge of the transgressions of the state in the spiritual realm.

This did not mean, however, that the Christian might loosely regard his obligations to the civil power. St. Augustine taught with no little force the Christian's obligation to serve when called upon in the military forces of Rome. His reasoning on the subject of the just war has influenced modern thinking to a great extent. He would also justify the use of the temporal power in the suppression of heresy—a practice of dubious value and unhappy consequences for both Church and society.

The barbarian invaders who were to destroy the authority of imperial Rome were attacking St. Augustine's see-city in Africa when the great saint died. The Gothic invasion had greatly weakened imperial authority in Italy. With the emperor now residing in Constantinople, the Church leaders in the west were asserting the independence of the Church with even greater vigor. Among the letters to the emperor of Pope Gelasius I toward the close of the fifth century, we find most explicit statements of the relationship of the spiritual and temporal powers. In one of these he says: "There are two chief powers by which this world is governed, August Emperor: the sacred authority of the prelates and the kingly power. Wherein the burden laid upon the priests is heavier, in that they will have to render an account at the divine judgement even for the kings of men. You know, most Clement Son, that although you are placed in rank above all the races of men, nevertheless you bow your neck in devoted submission to those who are set in charge of matters of religion. You look to them for the means of your own salvation. . . . So far as concerns the rule of public order, the leaders of religion themselves obey your laws, recognizing that the imperial authority has been conferred upon you from on high. . . . With how much greater zeal, then ought you to obey those who are set in charge of the sacred mysteries."[4] Again he writes: "They [i.e., the civil authorities] shrink from interference with religious matters, and recognize that these do not fall within the measure of their authority, which has been allotted to them for the judgement of human things not also for the control of divine things; how then can they claim jurisdiction over those men who are ministers of the divine things? . . . For Christ being mindful of human frailty, provided for a grand dispensation for the salvation of his people. He separated the kingly duties and powers from the priestly, according to different functions and dignity proper to each, wishing that his people should be preserved by a saving humility, and not again ensnared by human pride. Henceforth Christian Emperors should stand in need of priests for their eternal life, and priests for their part should employ the aid of the imperial government for the direction of temporal matters; to the end that spiritual employment might be removed from carnal diversions and that the soldier of the Lord might be as little as possible entangled in secular business, and that one involved in secular affairs might not be occupying the leadership of the Church. Thus it was sought to secure that both the orders might be humble since no man could combine eminence in both of them, and that the profession of each might be suited to the special aptitudes of those who follow it."[5]

The theories of Pope Gelasius played a significant role in the ensuing centuries in the struggle between the political and the ecclesiastical powers. Defenders of the case on either side made use of the Gelasian theory. The theory, of course, did not spell out in detail what were the practical limits of each sphere. According to the nature of each controversy, both defenders of the ecclesiastical power and of political power were able, in borderline instances especially, to argue on the basis of the teaching of Gelasius.

[4] Epistles 12–2, and R. W. and A. J. Carlyle, *A History of Medieval Political Theory in the West* (3rd edition; Edinburgh and London: W. Blackwood & Sons, 1930), Vol. I, p. 191.

[5] Tractatus II, IV; quoted by Carlyle, *op. cit.*, Vol. I, p. 190.

The decline of the Empire brought a gradual disappearance of civil authority in the west. The recurring invasions of the barbarian peoples with the ensuing disorder made necessary the assertion of some authority for the protection of life and property. In the anarchic situation that prevailed, the one authority that remained was the Church. Upon the shoulders of its prelates fell the authority once exercised by the civil power of Rome. The assumption of authority was gradual and for the most part accidental. It is true that even in the later days of the Empire, after Christianity had been recognized, churchmen frequently were commissioned to carry out secular functions. At one point in his life St. Augustine complains about the press of duties both civil and ecclesiastical. Some of these civil functions came to inhere in special bishoprics. The pagan invaders of the Roman lands held in a certain awe the Roman authority, even when the power that formerly sustained it had declined and disappeared. In addition, there was the spiritual power of the prelate, which frequently commanded an obedience which no other authority could command. The Church, therefore, bearer of Rome's power and culture, came to be both civil and religious ruler in these turbulent times. Such a situation brought both advantages and disadvantages. It meant a rapid spread of the civilizing force of Christianity; it established a certain peace, but it brought to the Church wealth and power, which had a corrupting influence upon churchmen and caused neglect of the Church's spiritual duties. So intertwined had temporal and religious functions in the hands of the Church become that when a few centuries later a reforming pope recommended a severance of all temporal functions of the Church, it was regarded as too idealistic a move even by the best of churchmen and civil rulers alike.

In the period between 600 and 800 it would be difficult to discern the separation of functions set forth by Gelasius. The civil authority was weak, kingdoms were in the process of formation, and the settling down of the people, so necessary for the stable life, was in the process of being realized. Nevertheless it is correct to say that older theories of the relation of the temporal to the spiritual authorities still held. Men believed in two separate authorities, each independent in its sphere. The churchman owed allegiance to the secular authority in secular matters;

the temporal authority owed allegiance to the ecclesiastical authority in matters spiritual. There was no repudiation of this theory. Such a leader as Pope St. Gregory the Great shows such a respect for the sacredness of temporal power that he condemns as unlawful and sacrilegious any rebellion against it. The extreme nature of his condemnation is readily explained by the all-too-ready tendency of our semi-barbaric ancestors to violence and rebellion. "Those," he says, "who murmur against the rulers set over them speak not against a human being, but against Him Who disposes all things to divine order."[6] Even wicked rulers should be obeyed as having been sent by God for the punishment of sin. In later centuries, Gregory the Great's theory on the sanctity of the temporal power was commonly used by anti-papalist writers against ecclesiastical power. Even a theory of divine right of rulers was read into his teachings, although it is difficult to find this theory as it was developed in the sixteenth and seventeenth centuries.

Following earlier writers Gregory accepts the theory that coercive government is a result of sin but at the same time a divine remedy. Does this mean if there were no sin there would be no need of government? Evidently not, for we are told: "The dispensation of divine providence established diverse ranks and distinct orders for this purpose: that while the less should show reverence for the more powerful and the more powerful should impose their will upon the less, one fabric of concord would be made from diversity and the administration of individual offices would be rightly performed. For a whole could in no way exist unless a great order of difference of this sort should preserve it. And the example of the celestial hosts shows that in truth created beings cannot be governed nor live in one and the same equality, because, since there are angels and archangels, it is clear that they are not equal, but one differs from the other in power and order, even as we do. If therefore, among these, who are without sin, there is established such distinction, what man will refuse to submit himself willingly to this disposition which he knows that even angels obey."[7]

Despite repeated warnings of the writers of this period that

[6] *Libri Moralium in Job*, Vol. 22, Ch. 24.
[7] *Epistolae*, Bk. 5, No. 59, quoted by Carlyle, *op. cit.*, Vol. I, p. 127.

the temporal authority is sacred and must be obeyed, writers have left an abundance of evidence that they entertained no illusion about the temptation to tyranny of the civil rulers. While the ruler is generally regarded as a judge of the law, he is warned in the words of St. Augustine: "It is not for judges to judge of the law but according to the law." It is said emphatically that a king is not a king if he does not rule according to the law. This is the condition on which he rules. Nor do the writers forget that the king has taken a sacred oath at his coronation to observe the divine law and the customs of his people. Isidore of Seville writes: "Kings are so called from ruling . . . thereby doing righteously the name of king is retained, by wrong doing it is lost. Wherefore this was a proverb among the ancients: 'You shall be king if you rule rightly; if you do not, you shall not be.' "[8] More emphatic are the words of one unknown chronicler of the time: "What are impious kings but the greater robbers of the earth, fierce as lions, ravening like wolves; but they are great today and perish tomorrow, and of them God has said, 'They reigned, but not by Me, they arose as princes, but I knew them not.' The evil ruler or tyrant is no true king; he is only as Cicero called him, a wild beast, the most terrible and loathsome known to the world."[9]

What picture of the just ruler is given to us? To sum up the attributes of a just king according to the writings of the time— he will judge righteously between men, he will defend the weak, he will punish the wicked, he will protect the Church, he will place honest administrators over the state's affairs, he will not oppress the people with heavy exactions, he will live in God according to the Catholic faith, and he will keep his children from evil. What can be done if he does not live according to these precepts or if he is an usurper? Here was the difficulty and the reason for the frequent recourse to violence. There existed little effective machinery to put the theories into practice. The one other source of power remained—the Church. Since the ruler took a sacred oath upon entering into office, the observance of

[8] *Etymologiae*, Bk. 9, Ch. 3; quoted in Ewart Lewis, *Medieval Political Ideas* (New York: Alfred A. Knopf, 1954.), Vol. I, p. 143.
[9] For a distinction between kings and tyrants in the ninth century writers, see Carlyle, *op. cit.*, Vol. I, Ch. XVIII, XIX.

his oath and of all the oaths was a concern of the spiritual power. It became then a question for the Church to determine whether perjury had been committed. If it had been committed, the chief weapon in the arsenal of the Church was brought forth—excommunication. When excommunication was applied, the king's subjects were automatically released from their allegiance.

In the patristic era, the right of the ecclesiastical authority to call upon the temporal authority of the enforcement of law had been upheld. In the early Middle Ages, St. Isidore accepts the theory. He writes: "Secular princes sometimes hold heights of power within the Church, that through that power they may strengthen ecclesiastical discipline. Powers would not be necessary within the Church were it not that what the priest cannot accomplish through the word of his teaching, the power may command through the terror of his discipline. The heavenly kingdom is often aided by the earthly kingdom, that those members of the Church who act against the faith and discipline of the Church may be destroyed by the forces of princes. . . . Let secular princes know that they are responsible to God for the Church which Christ has given to their protection."[10]

The restoration of the Empire in the west by Pope Leo I in 800, while strengthening the arm of the Church, brought other problems not unknown in earlier times. After the recognition of Christianity under Constantine the problem confronting the Church was how to preserve its independence in the face of a strong and well-established temporal power. Emperors did not hesitate to interfere directly in Church affairs despite the stubborn opposition of vigorous churchmen. Once again, for a time, a strong temporal authority had come into being. Some ecclesiasts, happy at the establishment of a strong power as guarantee of peace against civil anarchy, gave more than due veneration to the newly proclaimed emperor. In certain contemporary paintings Charlemagne wears the garments of a priest. And the old title of respect, "Vicar of God," is frequently used to describe his exalted position. His reign, however, was short, and at its end Europe fell once again into anarchy. Divided by factional strife, Europe fell an easy prey to further barbarian invasions. The

[10] *Sententiae*, Bk. 3, Ch. 51, sec. 4; quoted by E. Lewis, *op. cit.*, Vol. 1, p. 145.

Norsemen invaded the north and west; the Magyars the East. Both temporal and ecclesiastical authority were all but destroyed. The older civilization, however, survived and the conquerors succumbed to its influence. Among the invaders were the Normans. These people who settled in northwestern France made significant contributions of their own to European civilization.

While the immediate effect of the break-up of Charlemagne's empire was the strengthening of feudalism with its decentralizing tendencies, it also had the effect of preparing the foundations of those states of Europe which have become familiar to us today.

Conditions in the Church both in matters of faith and discipline, which had sunk to a low ebb in the ninth and tenth centuries, were greatly improved under a series of reforming popes, for the most part members of the monastic order of the Benedictines. Best known of the reforming popes is Gregory VII, known also as Hildebrand. Gregory faced a condition long established in practice—the investiture of bishops in their symbols of office (ring and crozier) by kings and emperors. Secular rulers insisted that bishops and abbots as temporal lords of great landholdings and as councillors of the royal and imperial courts must receive the approval of the temporal power. However logical the argument of the temporal rulers was, it did happen that frequently in practice kings and emperors filled the episcopal vacancies with little regard for canonical election by the clergy of a diocese. As a result many prelates were political appointees of the king, secular lords with little or no training or fitness for office.

All this Gregory sought to prevent. In 1075 he issued a decree prohibiting all lay investiture. The decree was far more radical than many reformers within the Church desired. They had hoped for some restrictions of the practice, knowing well that complete abolition of a practice now sanctioned by centuries of use could scarcely be accomplished. Gregory, however, was insistent that the independence of the Church required the complete abolition of lay investiture. No one could deny that theoretically he was correct, but such a sweeping reform as he sought ran counter to the whole social political and ecclesiastical framework of western Europe. To have been complete, it would have required renunciation of all temporal jurisdiction by bishops and abbots.

The struggle that ensued between Gregory and the Emperor Henry IV is one of the great dramas of history. For his refusal to obey the papal decree, Henry was excommunicated by the Pope and his subjects freed from obedience to him. At first victorious in the struggle, the Pope forced Henry to obedience in the famous submission of the Emperor at Canossa. Fortune turned, however, in favor of the Emperor, and Gregory died in exile.

The arguments of imperial and papal writers of the time cover the whole range of theory of the relations of the spiritual to the secular. Both sides are guilty of extreme claims generated by the very intensity of the conflict, but calmer reasoning may also be found in the documents of the time. Gregory at one point reminds the Emperor, "Who does not know that kings and rulers had their beginning in men inspired by the Devil, the prince of the world, to turn away from God and presume in the blindness of their lust and their intolerable arrogance to bear rule over men, their equals, through pride, violence, fraud, bloodshed, and almost every known crime?"[11] Henry tells Gregory: "You have laid hands upon me who, . . . as the tradition of the Holy Fathers teaches, am to be judged by God alone and not to be deposed for any crime unless I should wander from the faith, which God forbid."[12] The Emperor adds that the Fathers of the Church had not even deposed the apostate Julian.

The arguments on both sides were generally based on Gelasian principles. Gregory accepts the independence of the two powers. Professor McIlwain sums up Gregory's position thus: "Secular government is necessary and it is not in itself evil, but by nature the authority of the bishop is above it just as the spiritual part of man is superior to the carnal; it is divine in a higher sense than royal power because it is the direct instrument of God to fulfill his will, while man's wickedness was the occasion of the creation of all temporal rule though its cause might be God's ordinance. This did not mean that the pope was above the king in secular matters; it did not imply that the pope had any strictly secular authority whatever. The pope, in Gregory's view, was not temporal lord of the world, not even the Christian world. *He was*

---

[11] Letter of Gregory to the Bishop of Metz, 1081 *Registrum of Gregory VII.*
[12] Quoted in Carlyle, *op. cit.*, Vol. IV, p. 186, n. 1.

pastor of the flock of Christ. But as such it was his duty to see that the flock received no harm, and he must take any measures necessary for its defence and welfare. For such an end he might even depose a king or emperor and sanction the election of another, and had authority to release all subjects from their oaths and obligations."[13]

Behind the dispute lay certain historical factors which complicated the problem of clarification of views. The predecessors of Henry IV, notably Henry II, who had been canonized, had taken a lead in instituting reforms within the Church during the years preceding Gregory's coming to the papacy. The ecclesiastical rule of celibacy of the clergy had in certain areas fallen into disuse. In addition simony was not uncommon. While the emperors had an eye to the practical in enforcing clerical celibacy in that the unity of the Empire would be weakened by the holders of imperial fiefs handing on title to one or more heirs, yet they did aid the Church in the enforcement of the rule, the breach of which caused much scandal. On the other hand the special nature of the German law and custom under feudal practice provided that the owner of property had every right connected therewith. Such rights would include not only the ownership of the church or churches on his land but also the income from churches and the appointment of the priest or bishop in charge. The emperor considered all churches, especially cathedrals, as coming within his control. Undoubtedly Henry considered Gregory as coming within imperial jurisdiction when he deposed him as Bishop of Rome.[14]

From the writings of some of Gregory's defenders, certain ideas appear which throughout the following centuries exercise great influence in curbing the powers of kings. Thus Manegold of the monastery of Lautenbach in Alsace writes: "Therefore even as the royal dignity and authority excels all earthly authority, so no infamous or shameful man is appointed to administer it, but he who no less in wisdom, justice, and piety than in place and dignity is superior to others. Therefore it is necessary that he who

[13] Charles H. McIlwain, *The Growth of Political Thought in the West* (New York: The Macmillan Company, 1932), p. 208.
[14] An excellent account of the dispute between Henry & Gregory is found in H. Romen, *The State in Catholic Thought* (St. Louis: Herder Book Co., 1945).

is to bear the charge of all and govern all should shine above others in greater grace of the virtues. . . . For the people do not exalt him above themselves in order to grant him a free opportunity to exercise tyranny against them, but that he may defend them from the tyranny and unrighteousness of others. Yet when he who has been chosen for the coercion of the wicked and the defense of the upright has begun to foster evil against them, to destroy the good, and himself to exercise most cruelly against his subjects the tyranny which he ought to repel, is it not clear that he who deservedly falls from the dignity entrusted to him and that the people stand free of his lordship and subjection, when he has been evidently the first to break the compact for whose sake he was appointed?"[15]

The unknown author of the *York Tractates*, written in a similar dispute in England about 1100, gives the royal side of the case. He contends that the consecration of kings confers a divine authority. Even though a bishop consecrates, the divine character of kingship is not a gift of the bishop, but it is a gift of God. If it were true that consecration of the king by the bishops meant that the bishops were therefore superior to the king, then the cardinals of the Church would be superior to the pope inasmuch as they consecrate him. He contends that there is a divine nature both to the office of the bishop and to the office of the king. But he grants an over-all superiority to the king. Drawing from the Old and New Testament, he asserts that the king should have the power and rule over priests. "Therefore," he continues, "some venture to think among men likewise the royal power is greater and higher than the priest, as being the imitation or ideal of the better and more exalted nature of Christ (as king). And so they say that it is not against the justice of God if the priestly dignity is instituted by the royal and made subject to it, for with Christ it so happened that he was made priest through his own royal power and through his priesthood was made subject to the Father with whom in royal power He was equal.[16]

As for tyrants, the author of the *Tractates* contends that they do not rule through the grace of God, for they are not really kings. He leaves open the question of how a tyrant is to be re-

[15] From E. Lewis, *op. cit.*, Vol. I, p. 165.
[16] *Libelli de Lite*, Vol. III, p. 667; quoted in McIlwain, *op. cit.*, p. 213.

moved, the Church having been the most certain agency for their deposition. He seems nevertheless to question the very power of the papacy as such and his work is frequently said to foreshadow the ideas of the sixteenth century rather than mirroring the ideas of the twelfth. Yet it remains true that defenders of the imperial power frequently found themselves close to a denial of all papal power.

The argument, however, on the fundamental Gelasian principle of most parties to the dispute did not render the controversy any less bitter. It should be remembered that times were changing and events not clearly recognized by either party were taking shape. Kings and emperors were no longer barbarous, untutored rulers as they once had been. They had now begun to contend with the clergy as representatives of the new Christian civilization. As Professor McIlwain points out, Gregory was seeking no new power nor consciously contending that he rule as fully over the temporal as over the spiritual: ". . . The supremacy claimed for the Pope by the Gregorians as his right was a supremacy not based on a new conception of the *sacerdotium* or of the regnum, whether in fact or in the minds of the writers themselves, but based rather upon claims long made and now merely carried to their logical conclusion and defined in somewhat more clearcut terms; in other words, that Gregory was in reality 'standing upon the ancient ways' and can truly be called an innovator only in the practical application of his principles, not in the underlying principles themselves."[17] Gregory was asserting an old principle in his claim that within the Church kings and emperors could claim no position different from their fellow Christians when it came to the observance of divine or canon law. Hindsight now makes it clear to another day and age that he could not reasonably expect the emperor to surrender his control over prelates who exercised both temporal and spiritual power within his domains. Relinquishing all control of temporalities by the prelates would have, it was believed by churchmen, endangered the independence of the Church and would have been a violation of trust inasmuch as most of the landed wealth had come through the ages by deeds of gift. The law today is complicated enough on the breaking of long-outmoded bequests; it was even more

[17] McIlwain, *op. cit.*, p. 220.

so in the middle ages. The contest, therefore, was not, as some picture it, a contest of power-hungry prelates and kings; sincere and good men honestly differed on a question that finds even today no clear-cut practical solution.

In the twelfth century John of Salisbury, who had been secretary to the martyred Thomas à Becket, might sanction tyrannicide as the solution of royal lawlessness, but others were writing on a grand conception of unity of temporal and spiritual power. Stephen of Tournai in his *Summa Decreti* gave this account of Christian society: "In the same city, under the same king, there are two peoples, and for the two peoples there are two ways of life, and for the two ways of life there are two governments, and in accordance with these two governments there is a twofold order of jurisdiction. The City is the Church; the King of the City is Christ; the two peoples are the two orders in the Church, clerics and laymen; the two lines are the spiritual and the carnal; the two governments, the priestly and the regal; the twofold jurisdiction, divine and human law. Render to each its due, and all will be well."[18] Or as Professor Maitland puts it: "Then in the Middle Ages these thoughts at once issue in the postulate of an Eternal, Visible Community comprehending All mankind. In the Universal Whole, mankind is a partial whole with a final cause of its own, which is distinct from the final causes of Individuals and from those of other communities. Therefore in all centuries of the Middle Ages Christendom which in destiny is identical with mankind, is set before us as a single, universal Community, founded and governed by God himself. Mankind is one 'mystical body'; it is one single and internally connected 'people' or 'folk'; it is an all-embracing corporation [*universitas*], which constitutes the Universal Realm, spiritual and temporal, which may be called the Universal Church [*ecclesia universalis*], or, with equal propriety, the Commonwealth of the human Race [*respublica generis humani*]. Therefore that it may attain its one purpose, it needs one Law [*lex*] and One Government [*unius principatus*]."[19]

---

[18] Carlyle, *op. cit.*, Vol. II, p. 198.
[19] The translation by F. W. Maitland of *Das Deutsche Genossenschftsrecht* of Otto von Gierke under the title *Political Theories of the Middle Ages* (Cambridge, 1900), p. 10.

No more noble idea has ever captivated the mind of man. It was, however, a noble theory over which "the great parties of the Middle Ages fell a-fighting."[20] Dante in his sublime *De Monarchia* was to sing its swan song in the thirteenth century as the great nation states were coming into power to challenge universal empires—both spiritual and temporal. The spiritual power rose to its greatest heights under several able popes, able students of the canon law, who while adhering to older theories of the relation of the temporal to the spiritual power often claimed a wider jurisdiction than had hitherto been known. If it is the period of great popes, it is also the period of great theologians, the best known of whom is St. Thomas Aquinas. It is worthy of note that while related by blood to the Emperor Frederick II, who was frequently involved in disputes with the papacy, St. Thomas makes no mention in any of his works of the current papal-imperial quarrels. Inspired by the works of Aristotle, recently recovered, he gives us a political theory which adheres closely to the writings of that Greek philosopher.

The political order of St. Thomas is natural to man. It is not a remedy for sin, but as all things natural are God's creation, so is the political order. It is therefore both natural and sacred. The political order arises from the nature of man, who is a political and social being. Man could not exist without it. The political order and its agent the government while they correct evil are a force for good and would be necessary even in a society of angels. Therefore unlike the eighteenth-century theorists, St. Thomas does not believe that government is a necessary evil. Nor does he believe that it is simply a negative force for the preservation of peace; rather, he believes that it is a positive force for the promotion of man's welfare. The political order resulting from God's design and stemming from God as its source assumes a position of heightened prestige and dignity. Its end is the common good of man in the promotion of the natural virtues and caring for temporal needs.

Beyond the temporal end of man is his ultimate end, and so St. Thomas says: "Now there is a certain good, extraneous to man as long as he is in this mortal life: namely, the ultimate

[20] Maitland, *op. cit.*, p. 11.

beatitude which he hopes for after death in the enjoyment of God. . . . Whence the Christian man, for whom that beatitude has been won by the blood of Christ, and who to seek it has received the Holy Spirit as a pledge, needs another spiritual office by which he may be guided to the harbor of eternal salvation, and this office is performed for the faithful by the ministers of the Church. . . . But if, indeed, they [men] could attain this end [enjoyment of God] by the virtue of human nature, it would necessarily belong to the office of king to direct men to this end. For we suppose him to be king, to whom the height of rule in human things is committed. . . . But because man does not attain the end of enjoyment of God through human virtue but by divine virtue . . . therefore to guide men to that end will not belong to human government, but to divine. . . . Therefore in order that spiritual things might be distinct from earthly things, the ministry of that government was not committed to earthly kings but to priests and especially to the highest priest, the successor of Peter, the Roman Pontiff, Vicar of Christ, to whom all the kings of the Christian people ought to be subject, as they are to our Lord Jesus Christ. For thus those to whom belongs the care of antecedent ends ought to be subject to him to whom the care of the ultimate end belongs, and to be directed by his command."[21]

The temporal power should, furthermore, do all within its power to direct men to their supernatural end and should be guided in this by the spiritual power. The temporal power should prescribe those things that lead to supernatural happiness and should forbid those things that divert man from it. Thus in spiritual things the temporal power is an agent of the spiritual power. In other words, the temporal order not only aids the Church in securing man's ultimate end, but defends it against its enemies. St. Thomas proposes peaceful and continuous cooperation.

He would maintain that the popes could excommunicate a ruler who disregarded the Divine and Church laws or who had lapsed into heresy, thus relieving his subjects of the obligation of obedience. At the same time Christians must obey a non-

[21] *De Regimen Principum*, Bk. I, Ch. XIV.

Catholic ruler who had never been a Catholic. They should, however, try to prevent the setting up of such a rule where possible.

St. Thomas may not be classed with those writers of his age who believed that all power is mediated through the pope or who maintained that there exists a plenitude of power in the pope over all things temporal and spiritual. He occupies a more moderate position. His teachings seem to be in accord with supporters of the theory of indirect power recognizing a fullness of temporal power in the king and only when necessity requires an interference in temporal affairs by the ecclesiastical power. He is firm in his insistence that the spiritual power must obey the temporal power in matters that involve the temporal common good. In one of his early works, however, after having cited the necessity for obedience in temporal affairs to the temporal rulers, he adds: ". . . unless perchance the secular power is joined with the spiritual as in the Pope who stands at the top of both."[22] Considering the general tenor of St. Thomas's writings on the subject, the sentence seems paradoxical. St. Robert Bellarmine suggested later that it applied solely to the states of the Church. Later writers such as Carlyle suggested that it represents an early view which St. Thomas later revised.

The canon lawyers of the period, sometimes known as the Decretalists, held to a more extreme view of papal power. Influenced by the idea of corporation taken from Roman law, they thought of the Church in corporative terms. The Church was a corporation embracing all phases of life, with the pope as the supreme head of the body. Most of the canonists in following the path of lawyers were generally strict constructionists and legalistic in their approach. The extreme claims of some of the popes of the period, notably Innocent III and Innocent IV, may be explained by the fact that they were canon lawyers and represented the point of view of the professionals. An old Chinese maxim says: "When two men ride a horse, one must ride behind," which describes a situation confronting controversialists of the Middle Ages. Canonists placed the pope at the head; theologians seemed to be satisfied with the fact that the two riders rode at the same level, each with full command of the place occupied.

[22] Commentary on the Sentences of Peter Lombard, II D. 44, Q. 2, Art. 3.

One of the most prominent of the canonists, Hostiensis, taught that the emperor held his power from the Roman Church and could be called its vicar. Carlyle describes the position of Hostiensis as follows: "The spiritual power is superior to the earthly on three points: in dignity, for the spirit is greater and more honorable than the body; in time, for it was earlier; and in power, for it not only institutes the temporal power but also has authority to judge it, while the Pope cannot be judged by any man, except in case of heresy. . . . For the Pope receives from God alone the authority of the earthly and heavenly empire."[23] Pope Innocent III, while recognizing a distinction between the temporal and the spiritual and the right of authorities in each sphere to exercise their special powers, claims that it is for him to decide when uncertain matters belong to one sphere or to the other. It is the emphasis which Innocent places upon his words, however, rather than a change of traditional theory that has given him the reputation of an extreme claimant of papal power. He speaks of himself as placed above all peoples and endowed with full power, judging all men but judged by God alone. He claims a fullness of spiritual power and a latitude of temporal power. Yet in practice he does not desire complete control of all things. When the Count of Montpellier asked him to declare legitimate the Count's illegitimate children, the Pope refused on the ground that the Holy See will undertake a step where qualifications for spiritual office are concerned but not for secular purposes. He contends that this is a matter of the king of France to decide.

The singular activity of the popes in the twelfth and thirteenth centuries was in no small measure caused by the increasing warlike activities between the new nation states and the pope's role as arbiter between the conflicting claims of the rulers. In one of the many conflicts between the king of France and the king of England we find Pope Innocent III saying after reciting the horrors of war: "Therefore let no one think that we intend to infringe upon or diminish the jurisdiction and authority of the illustrious King of France, since he neither would nor should infringe upon our own jurisdiction . . . but . . . since the King of England, as he asserts, is sufficiently prepared to show that the

[23] Carlyle, *op. cit.*, Vol. V, p. 329.

King of France sinned against him . . . how can we, who have been called by supernatural disposition to the government of the Universal Church, fail to heed the divine mandate? . . . For we do not intend to judge concerning the fief which lies in his jurisdiction . . . but to judge concerning the sin, for this, without doubt we have judgment which we can and ought to exercise on anyone whomever."[24]

1117726

Pope Innocent III never claimed a full temporal jurisdiction. His successor, Innocent IV, also a canon lawyer, appears to have claimed a much wider jurisdiction than his predecessor. He claimed a pontifical and regal power and he insisted that the pope was the ordinary judge of all men. As Mrs. Lewis puts it: "The Pope had the power to depose emperors and kings, to appoint an emperor when the electors were negligent, to hear appeals from a secular court in case of defect of jurisdiction, and to appoint a guardian for a kingdom whose king was unable to preserve peace and justice. In short he thought of the Pope as the normal superior of all temporal power."[25]

By the fourteenth century, the dispute revolved around the question not so much of prestige but of power. It had formerly been argued on the basis of the Gelasian principle that there were two powers, ordained by God, but that ecclesiastical power occupied a position of greater prestige. The question now turned upon the determination of which power ruled the other. The significant work on behalf of the temporal power is written by John of Jandun and Marsiglio of Padua. The *Defensor Pacis* of these two authors appeared about 1324 in defense of Lewis of Bavaria in his struggle with Pope John XXII. It is not known to whom we owe the larger portion of the work, but ordinarily Marsiglio is referred to most frequently as the major author.

Marsiglio adopts as his starting point Aristotle's view that the state is a natural whole composed of certain parts—agriculturists, artisans, warriors, financial officials, and the priesthood. Men naturally fall under one of these classes. But the efficient cause or power that creates them and separates them is a *legislator humanus*. The same power establishes the *pars principans* "to regulate the political and civil acts of men." The *legislator*

[24] *Decretal Novit*, quoted in E. L. Lewis, *op. cit.*, pp. 524-25.
[25] Lewis *op. cit.*, p. 526.

humanus does not correspond to a modern legislature. Marsiglio declares that "the legislator, or prime and proper effective cause of law" is the *populus* or body of citizens or the dominant portion thereof. "I say," he continues, "the dominant portion having in mind the number and the quality of the persons in the community for which the law is enacted."[26] He makes use of a maxim of Roman private law which had been incorporated in canon law, *"Quod omnes tangit debet ab omnibus approbari"* ("What touches all must be approved by all." The phrase comes from regulations concerning the making of wills in the Justinian code. It is frequently found in medieval documents), Marsiglio contends: "The things that may touch the advantage and disadvantage of all ought to be known and heard by all."[27] It will be noted that the *legislator humanus* takes account of both quality and quantity. Professor McIlwain says of this legislative body: "In fact this is not a modern touch at all, it is strictly medieval in character and antique in origin, corresponding in its nature much more closely to the *maior and sanior* parts of a cathedral chapter which took account of quality as well as number, in determining the election of a medieval bishop."[28]

It is not the modern legislature in its action. Medieval times did not know of a legislating body putting forth volumes of statutes. It was generally assumed that law was *discovered* and not *made*. The *legislator humanus* would seem to be more like our constitutional conventions for setting up a structure of government. The executive or royal power appears from Marsiglio's work to be the king which the Middle Ages knew—a monarch with full governing authority in whom judicial power was also lodged.

The radical and original part of the *Defensor Pacis* deals with the Church and the political order. Holding to the idea common in his day that there is one *Respublica Christiana*—one Christian Commonwealth which comprises both the empire and the Church —he equates the whole body of Christians with the "people" who have final power and authority. He defines the Church as "the body of the faithful believing in and calling upon the name

[26] *Defensor Pacis*, I, XII, 3.
[27] *Ibid.* I, XII, 6.
[28] McIlwain, *op. cit.*, p. 303.

of Christ."[29] From the body of the faithful flows all power—political and ecclesiastical. The faithful have two powers—elective and legislative. They nominate and select bishops and parish priests. Their legislative power consists in laying down rules for the Church and clergy, and in general council deciding the meaning of Scriptures. The spiritual power comes from God and consists in the power of administering the sacraments. The power is equal in all priests and any priest may communicate the power to persons legitimately selected by the community. He argues that the Church has no visible head and that St. Peter received no more power than any other apostle. The pope according to Marsiglio is an administrative head of the Church; he may call councils but the councils are superior to him. All ecclesiastical power proceeds from the community, or from the emperor who has his authority from the people. The Church may not possess material goods, or legislate, or exercise any power without authorization from the state. The pope possesses no power over any man except with the emperor's permission. The Church, therefore, is but a department of the state. In 1327 Marsiglio and his work were condemned by Pope John XXII.

By the fourteenth century, it was becoming more evident that the idea of a universal empire was being challenged more and more successfully by the new nation states. With the challenge to the empire went a challenge to the universal Church. The cherished medieval concept of unity, spiritual and temporal, had lost its hold on the minds of men. Some centuries remained before the spiritual unity would be broken, but unity of the temporal powers was giving place to the idea of unity within the separate states. Kings were bringing independent nobles and independent communities within their realms under centralized power.

With tragic results for the Church, Boniface VIII met head-on the power of France, "eldest daughter of the Church." The dispute arose, as so many had in this period, over the efforts of the Pope to bring peace, first between England and Scotland, and second, between the old rivals England and France. Involved were all those questions that had arisen before—the right of the king to tax church property, the privileged position of the clergy

[29] *Defensor Pacis*, II, II, 3.

within the realm, the interference of the Church in disputes between monarchs where sin was involved, and, as usual, the power of excommunication and its effects. Philip the Fair, king of France, with his legal advisers challenged Pope Boniface on all counts. On neither side did there appear to be any recognition of the new forces now shaping the destiny of the world—particularly the force of nationalism. Boniface, a good but stern scholar, without imagination, did not seem to realize the force of nationalistic tendencies nor the new power of the educated rulers. Philip's ambition blinded him even to the justice of many of the claims against him.

The most moderate of the King's defenders was John of Paris, a Dominican theologian who based his arguments on the philosophy of St. Thomas.[30] John accepts the Gelasian principle of the two powers but goes on to say that the *regnum* or state is a natural institution which has its roots in man's nature to satisfy his temporal needs and to provide for the common good. The Church is supernatural, directing men to beatitude in the life hereafter. The powers of both come from God. The primacy of the spiritual, however, is purely a spiritual primacy, a primacy of prestige. The Church is a visible *regnum* and may possess material goods, contrary to the teaching of the Waldensians, but its jurisdiction is spiritual and does not entail a temporal jurisdiction. He calls it *regnum sacerdotale*. It represents primarily the order of grace and not of nature. On the other hand the state is a natural institution for temporal ends and its power is not mediated through the Church. The temporal authority, it is true, has a moral function, since the relationship of politics to morals is very close. Fundamentally questions of justice and law are moral questions. It is true that one's temporal existence may not be wholly set apart from one's supernatural end, but the state has no direct power in the spiritual sense. The ruler is a member of the Church (or so he was in John's day) and subject to its spiritual directions. John, nevertheless, contends that the state may not be used by the spiritual power to accomplish its ends. If the Church corrects the ruler for a spiritual fault or excommunicates him, it is treating him as any son of the Church would

[30] *Tractato de Potestate Regia et Papali,* 1302.

be treated in like circumstances, and it is not responsible for the political consequences which the spiritual means entail. Finally, whatever temporal dominion the pope has, he possesses not as Vicar of Christ but as a concession of lay rulers.

The papal case in the debate is stated extensively by Aegidius Romanus. All power, he contends, comes from God through the Church. While the Church does not have immediate jurisdiction in temporal things it has a primary dominion. Spiritual power takes precedence over temporal power, so the power of the prince is secondary. Over temporal things the ruler has a right of use. Professor McIlwain, paraphrasing Aegidius, put it this way: "Therefore we do not claim that Caesar has no *dominium utile* (right of use) in temporal matters, but we do claim that the Church is higher and that Caesar's right ought to be disposed according to the right of the Church. We do not even say that Caesar has no directive power or jurisdiction over the persons of men or their temporal goods. We do say that the Church's directive power is far higher than Caesar's since she has the power to judge of the person of Caesar and of his temporal goods and can even reach his person by ecclesiastical censures, and can hand over his goods to the dominion of another."[31] Aegidius insists that it is through the Church that men hold any power. No person, he would say, has a right to an inheritance or anything else except he be baptized. Since the Church baptizes, it confers the right. A similar argument, it will be recalled, was used during the investiture controversy, when some claimed that inasmuch as the Church consecrated the emperor at coronation, his power comes from the Church. Aegidius' arguments, along with the arguments of the canon lawyers of his time, represent the high point of the papal claim.

The position of Pope Boniface in the controversy is less extreme than his defenders, but his words in France are interpreted as claims of direct authority in temporal matters. In a letter of the French clergy to Boniface his claims are called "wonderful, novel, and unheard of."[32] The Pope is led to assert, "for forty years now we have been trained in law, and we know that there are two powers ordained by God. Who then ought to believe or can

[31] McIlwain, *op. cit.*, pp. 254-55.
[32] Quoted in McIlwain, *op. cit.*, p. 244, from Dupuy Preuves, p. 68.

believe that such fatuity, such folly ever entered our head? We declare that in nothing are we working to usurp the jurisdiction of the King of France. . . . The King cannot deny, nor any other of the faithful whosover he is that he is subject to us on the ground of sin."[33] The position of Boniface would have been made more clear by the addition of a few qualifying phrases in his letter as indicated by the famous sentence in the Bull *Unam Sanctam* when he states: "Moreover we declare, we affirm, we define, and pronounce that for every human creature it is absolutely necessary for salvation to be subject to the Roman Pontiff." What clarifications this has required from Catholics ever since!

The controversy between Philip and Boniface had become so bitter that the underlying bases for the dispute were lost sight of or at least not judiciously stated. Philip was excommunicated without any effect on his subjects, while Boniface, grossly humiliated in his own apartments in Anagni by French soldiery, died within hours of this affront to his dignity.

Fortune rather than determined policy brought the papacy under the influence of France. The successor to Boniface, the saintly Benedict XI, lived but a few months after his election. His successor, Clement V, formerly archbishop of Bordeaux, took up residence at Avignon in 1309, four years after his election. It was to be a temporary residence because of the public disorder at Rome, but it was destined to be the seat of the papacy for almost seventy years (1309–77). Clement, however, showed himself deferential to the French in his creation of cardinals. Of the twenty-four that he created, twenty-two were Frenchmen. He also established a custom of nepotism in appointments and privileges which plagued the papacy for generations.

The mischief of French influence bore its fruits when the pope returned to Rome, and the nationalistic efforts to control the head of the Church resulted in the Great Schism (1379–1417). Two contending popes and then three led not only to scandal, confusion, and relaxed discipline but to the determination on the part of sincere Catholics to seek drastic means for reform. The disputes in the Councils of Constance and Basle were not so much concerned with Church-state relations as with the internal

[33] Quoted in McIlwain, *op. cit.,* p. 79.

government of the Church. With the election of Martin V in 1417 the Schism was brought to an end at the Council of Constance, but irreparable harm had been done to the Church.

Within a century (1510) the Reformation had broken out and new problems of the relations of the Church and state had arisen. The immediate effect of the breaking apart of Christendom was to increase greatly the power of the secular rulers. Both the leaders of the reformed group and the leaders of the Catholic cause sought the protection of the temporal arm. Both parties not only sought protection, but asked that vigorous steps be taken by the temporal authority to stamp out defection in its ranks. In Protestant regions rulers no longer finding an over-all spiritual power to guide and curb them assumed the double role of head of the state and head of the church. In the Catholic lands, although according to the tenets of the Church no ruler could call himself head of the Church, rulers nevertheless were not loathe to act in this capacity. The turbulence of the time called for strong coercive measures, and they were forthcoming without hesitation. The Renaissance had already had the effect of strengthening the secular power. Emphasizing the glories of imperial Rome, it had the effect of glorifying and enhancing the splendor and prestige of the royal courts. The child of the Renaissance wanted peace for the pursuit of learning, and he found it in the strong centralized control of the monarchs.

Of the Reformation one authority writes: "What we call the Reformation was in one aspect, the definitive triumph of secular authority in a struggle with the Church already centuries old. In one country after another, the secular government established its local control of the Church, absorbing in the process much, at least, of its property and jurisdiction. In city after city, from Straslund to Geneva, the Reformation appears as the last act of an age-long conflict between city and Bishop. Even in Catholic countries the same thing happened in some degree. When Francis I secured from the Pope in 1516 the right to appoint his own bishops and by the ordinance of Villers Caterets in 1537, curtailed ecclesiastical jurisdiction, he was doing as far as he could what Henry VIII did in England. Ferdinand of Austria, like the Protestant Princes of North Germany, dissolved monasteries and appropriated the property. In Spain the Inquisition set up by the King in defiance of the Pope, was, among other things, a royal instrument for the control of the clergy. The Reformation was part of the process by which Europe was re-solved into a series of independent, secular, sovereign States."[34]

Looking at the political thought of the man who sparked the Reformation, it is difficult to find a consistent view of Church-state relations. For the most part, Martin Luther's thought was not political, whatever its political consequences. One may find a view of the Church, but not a view of the state. Luther spoke for the moment and for the special crisis that confronted him, consequently one finds varying and sometimes contradictory statements. His early view on the authority of princes appears to be less emphatic than his later views. He has often been ac-cused of being the promoter of state absolutism, but it is ques-tionable if he would have understood what the phrase meant. His views on the position of the ruler and his authority could have been borrowed from any number of medieval writers. Thus he tells us that the power of the ruler is of God and that no mat-ter how wicked he may be, resistance to him is never justified. At the same time the ruler is bound by divine and natural law. These bodies of law are primary. For positive law he seems to have little use, whether it was the Justinian Code or the canon law. Man-made law as well as human institutions are full of imperfections. Law, for him, consists essentially in the Scriptures and in the conscience of man.

He conceded that most princes were fools and rogues, but nevertheless they represented God. "The hand that wields the secular sword," he tells us, "is not a human hand, but the hand of God. It is God, not man, who hangs and breaks on the wheel, decapitates, and flogs: it is God who wages war."[35] Resistance to princes may be passive, as when they command what is contrary to the Scriptures, and the true Christian will choose martyrdom.

What is the Church? The Church consists of those who know God's will and do it. Its authority is purely spiritual. As Professor Allen says: "So absolutely did he distinguish the spiritual and the temporal that the realm of the spiritual vanished from sight.

[34] J. W. Allen, *Political Thought in the Sixteenth Century* (New York, Dial Press, 1928), pp. XIII–XIV.
[35] *Ob Kriegsleute*, 1526, ed. Weimar, XIX, p. 626.

Every earthly manifestation of the spiritual life of Christians, words, deeds, or intentions, are temporal things and within the jurisdiction of the temporal magistrate . . . but so far as it [the Church] is visible, it is a temporal thing. It is the duty of all secular princes to establish and maintain such Churches. . . . He [the Prince] may, therefore, dispose of existing Church property as seems best to him, he may appoint to benefice, he may deprive the clergy of all special jurisdiction."[36] For Luther, the clergy were entitled to no special privileges. The temporal power existed to punish the wicked whether they were clergy or not. The secular ruler could also undertake the reform of the Church. Unquestionably this constituted an open invitation to the temporal power to move in, which it showed no hesitancy in doing.

Could the temporal arm be used for spiritual purposes? Luther seems to give two answers. On the one hand, we have statements such as the following: "Therefore it is futile and impossible to command or to force any man to believe this or that. . . . Thus it is each man's own business what he believes; and he must see to it that he believes aright." Or "Heresy can never be contained by force. . . . It is God's word that must do the fighting; if that avail not, then it will remain unchecked by temporal powers, though they fill the world with blood."[37] And yet he calls upon the elector of Saxony in 1523 to put down by force the celebration of the Mass. In 1525 he insisted that the ruler must put down by force the activities of the Anabaptists and later he called for severe measures against Catholics. In 1533 he flatly declared that it is the duty of the secular magistrate to use the sword to put down false doctrine and worship. Yet in a sermon two weeks before he died, he declared that it is futile to use force against heretics "for by human force can we never dispel them, or make them other than what they are."[38]

For the other leading figure of the Reformation, John Calvin, the state exists "that idolatry, blasphemy of the name of God and against his truth and other scandal to religion, be not publicly set forth and broadcast among the people; that public peace be not troubled, that each be secured in what is his own, that

[36] J. W. Allen, *op. cit.*, p. 24.
[37] *Von Weltlicher Uberkeyt*, 1523.
[38] Quoted in J. W. Allen, *op. cit.*, from *Works*, Erlanger, Vol. XVI.

man's intercourse may be without fraud or violence, in fine that among Christians there may be some public and visible form of religion and that humanity be settled among men."[39]

With an emphasis that the papal defenders might have used in the times of Pope Innocent III, Calvin insisted that there are two powers ordained of God—spiritual and temporal—and each has its separate sphere, but that there must be an authority to define the truth and to say what heresy is and that authority can only be the church. What is the church? The true church—universal and visible—consists of those who hear, believe, and follow the word of God. Every good member of the church possessing the gift of the Holy Spirit is a guarantee that the church cannot err. The church, however, does not seem to speak with a collective voice, but every local church based on the word of God has the authority of the universal church. He believes that the Scriptures clearly give the outline of the organization of a church. But a local church may speak with great authority as it did at Geneva.

He grants that the church has no sword and no prisons, but it must establish and maintain proper discipline within a community. It must, therefore, have access to means of coercion. In a well-ordered community it must depend on the civil magistrate. The ruler himself, being a member of the church, must listen to it and follow its commands. He is no different from any other member. From this Professor Sabine concludes: "In practice, wherever possible, Calvinist government placed the two swords of Christian tradition in the Church, and gave the direction of the secular authority to the clergy rather than to secular rulers. The result was likely to be an intolerable rule of the saints: a meticulous regulation of the most private concern founded upon universal espionage, with only a shadowy distinction between the maintenance of public order, the control of private morals, and the preservation of pure doctrine and worship."[40] In fact the control of the church at Geneva over the private lives of the people was far more extensive than ever exercised in the Middle Ages.

[39] *Institutions de la Religion Chretienne*, Ed. Lefranc, p. 755.
[40] George H. Sabine, A History of Poltical Theory, (New York: Henry Holt & Co., Inc., 1949), p. 363.

Calvin preached and wrote with great emphasis against any kind of violent resistance to civil rulers. To him the state is an institution constituted by God himself for the sake of man's good. It is not a product of human reason or will. The people must obey civil power as if the prince were God. "It comes not of the perversity of man that kings and other lords have power upon the earth: but it comes of the providence and holy ordinance of God whom it has pleased to manage in this fashion the government of men."[41] Rulers are the vicars of God. So civil government is not of the natural law, as St. Thomas had thought, but of the divine law. It makes no difference what kind of ruler may hold the power; be he wicked, believer or nonbeliever, gentle or brutal, generous or greedy, just or arbitrary, he must be obeyed. There can be no justifiable rebellion against established authority. The ruler is responsible to God alone. Martyrdom alone is open to the Christian who refuses to obey a tyrannical and ungodly ruler. In the light of the aggressively rebellious actions of John Knox and other followers of Calvin, this doctrine sounds strange indeed. The Stuart kings of England were better Calvinists than the inheritors of the Calvinist tradition who opposed them.

Following the period of the Reformation came an era of national churches. The idea prevailed that one faith should prevail in the state in order that political stability be assured. No tolerance was extended to dissenters. The maxim *cujus regio ejus religio* generally prevailed. The ruler was to all intents and purposes head of both state and church. Even in Catholic lands, the pope's jurisdiction was confined to teaching the faithful. In Protestant England the Book of Canons (1640) described the position of the king in the following words: "The most high and sacred order of Kings is of divine right, being the ordinance of God himself, founded in the laws of nature and clearly established by express texts both of the Old and New Testaments." In France it was declared: "The King of France is in his kingdom like a bodily God." The kings merging both divine and temporal power were indeed absolute.

Paul Foster describes this period of the nation-state wherein Catholicism was the official religion: "In Spain the Kings ex-

[41] *Institute,* 1541, Ed. Lefranc, p. 756.

cluded the publication of Papal Bulls unless they had previously received royal assent, kept the Inquisition completely under their control, and for many centuries virtually appointed all bishops to their sees. In Austria, at a later date, the Emperor Joseph II took a most intransigent attitude to the Papacy. The situation was not made easier by the claims of such countries, that, as they were officially Catholic, the Church should support their policies . . . which they maintained were *ipso facto* Catholic policies. The vehement hostility of France and Spain, the two most important Catholic powers, the alliances of Cardinal Statesman Richelieu with the Protestant Gustavus Adolphus against the Catholic Hapsburgs, served to complicate the matter still further."[42]

For centuries, even to our own days, the Catholic Church suffered from the Church-state alliances. What gains there were from such an association were dearly paid for. Politically-minded churchmen served the state with more zeal than they served the Church. Churchmen obtaining their regular support from the state grew lazy in performance of the duties for which they were ordained. When the governments came into disrepute with the surge of popular movements, the Church too went down and with it the souls of many people. The difficulties of the Church in lands formerly held by Spain provides sad testimony of the consequences of the close alliance between the temporal and the spiritual. The bitter anticlericalism of the Latin lands, whatever else its cause, springs in no large part from this source. The veneer of Catholicism which coats many parts of the Latin world rub off easily against the forces of the modern world.

The divine absolution of the sixteenth century was challenged by a group of Catholic and Protestant writers known as the Monarchomachi; Dominicans and Jesuits among the Catholics and Calvinists among the Protestants based their theories on the idea of power descending from God through the people or upon the idea of all government being the result of a primitive contract between king and people. As a rule these writers did not defend religious tolerance. Toleration as public policy was upheld by certain small religious sects and by leaders of the com-

---

[42] Paul Foster, O. P., *Two Cities, A Study of Church-State Conflict* (Westminster, Md.: The Newman Press, 1955), pp. 78-79.

mercial classes who abhorred the disorder of the religious wars.

Among Catholic writers the most noteworthy theories of Church and state are put forward by Robert Cardinal Bellarmine and Francisco Suarez. While frequently using the terminology of the medieval writers, their theories of the indirect power of the pope define much more sharply than had hitherto been done the relation of the temporal to the spiritual. Moreover they live in an age when the existence of strong nation states is an undoubted fact and when the relationship of these states to conquered lands of primitive peoples becomes of the greatest importance.

These writers insist that the Church is a divine institution, founded by Christ Himself for the redemption of man. The Church is a perfect society having for its specific end the salvation of souls. The organization of the Church, with the pope as successor of St. Peter, is of divine origin. The power of the temporal order comes from God through the people, who may institute any form of government for the promotion of the common good. The ruler does not occupy his position by divine selection or right. The Church, considering its end or purpose, occupies a position of greater prestige and dignity than the state. The Church's end being spiritual, however, the pope has no direct power in the temporal order. He may exercise such a power in the domain over which he presides. All Catholics everywhere are subject to his guidance and direction in matters of faith and morals—whether they are rulers or citizens. He may dispense Catholics from their allegiance to a Catholic king or ruler who turns heretic, if he obstructs the practice of the faith or interferes with the freedom of the Church. Such action, however, will follow only after a judicial proceeding according to canon law and will be an extraordinary occasion, not a frequent occurrence. Proceedings of this kind would be instituted in Catholic states whose rulers were Catholic and whose citizens were all for the most part Catholic.

If the state is not Catholic in this sense, its citizens are obviously not subject either to the pope or to canon law. The political order is then under natural law. According to Suarez such a state should permit missionaries to enter, should protect the nationals of other states, and should not permit acts contrary to natural law—but these restrictions he places on the basis of international law.

Bellarmine and Suarez still wrote under the shadow of the Reformation. They hoped for a return of all Christians to the Catholic Church. They considered all baptized persons as subjects to the Church even if they had lapsed into heresy. Members of the various Protestant sects were looked upon by them as heretics in the strict sense. Such a view of Protestants today would not be held, despite the fact that their doctrines would he held heretical.

The modern age has seen many forms and varieties of relationship between Church and state. Names of famous philosophers have been associated with ideas looking toward the establishment of national, secular religions. Such people as Rousseau, Fichte, and Comte can be numbered among them. People of such a mind would set up a "patriotic God" and a religion that would serve the state's purpose and be subject entirely to the directions of the temporal order. The world has seen substitute secular religions such as nazism and communism challenge the very foundation of Christianity. On the other hand, various relationships between Chruch and state have come to be a part of the constitutional arrangements of many states. One type of Christianity or another is recognized as official in many states of the west. The official recognition may be no more than an acknowledgment of the prestige of one Christian group and its acceptance for all public functions. The relationship may be much closer, involving financial support for the established Church and various restrictions upon the practice of other religions. Toleration varies from complete freedom for all groups to restriction on all but the followers of the official religion. In most western countries, some form of public aid is given to the private religious schools of different religious groups.

The religiously neutral state is a development of the past century and a half. Neutrality generally means that a special recognition is given to no one religious group. The state declares freedom for all religious groups but in effect declares its incompetence to pronounce upon the truth of any one of them. Neutrality may comprehend a latent hostility toward religion—as was the case in France—or a benevolent attitude in which a respect for religions is evident in official acts—as in the United States. Separation of Church and state as a doctrine of strict application is well-nigh impossible in a social situation where the dominant part of the population adheres to religion and where many public questions are questions of morals as well as politics. To one adhering to the Judaic-Christian tradition, God is always to be obeyed rather than man, and protest, organized and vocal, will overcome any doctrinaire positions on separation of Church and state when the temporal authorities transgress divine or moral law. Religious people expect the temporal authority to respect both.

The purpose in reviewing at some length the centuries-long struggle between the temporal and the spiritual in the western world is not to illustrate a power struggle as such. Formerly it had been the custom of teachers of the history of the middle ages to concentrate on two things: the eccentricity of the time and the desire of power-hungry popes to dominate the world for the purpose of keeping it in a state of darkness. To emphasize the eccentricity of any age is not to teach history. Five hundred years from now, describing our own age, a teacher might emphasize the automobile massacre on the highways, juvenile delinquency, divorce making it possible for a man to have five or six wives, men sitting on the top of flagpoles to establish endurance records, students crowding into telephone booths which are not even equipped with telephones, or, more seriously, the blood bath of the twentieth century with all its horrors of war and the cruelty of the concentration camps. If Mr. Khrushchev is right and the world should become Communist, the teacher will also tell of the power-hungry leaders of the democratic states who sought to subvert the world for the sole purpose of economic domination.

The overwhelming task that the Church faced with the decline of Roman civil power should never be lost sight of. Our ancestors were warlike, primitive, and not easily tamed. To bring them to the practice and understanding of Christ-like virtues required fortitude and missionary zeal such as the modern world has seldom seen. Whatever some moderns may think about the age of "organized religion," it can truthfully be said that had Christianity not been organized in those early days, it might well have been swallowed up in the high tides of the barbarian invasions. It was organized in structure and belief, and all succeeding ages owe a debt of gratitude to its civilizing force. The Church had no alternative but to perform both religious and civil tasks. Its involvement in the civil side of life was both inevitable and necessary. When the great revival of learning came in the twelfth and thirteenth centuries and the fusion of Greek, Roman, and Christian civilization had taken place, the Church had been the main agent in the creation of a new day and outlook on life. The great universities, products of its own zeal, were turning out those scholars who were to establish many of the most valued theories of political and social life so cherished by the modern age. It was now educating the lay statesmen who in turn were to govern the new nation-states. No doubt in so doing it was creating the new class which was to challenge its power in the political sphere. Perhaps churchmen and canonists were slow to realize that no longer was it necessary for the Church to hold securely the two swords of power—temporal and spiritual alike. The political order now able fully to undertake the task of temporal government with its own educated leaders no longer required the tutelage of the Church, so necessary in an earlier age.

In the over-all picture, it is the prudence of great popes, not the sincerity or the rectitude of causes they championed, that one may question. They were men of their age, as all of us are, and they sometimes failed to see the new forces making for change in their society. For the most part it was the independence of the Church they fought for. However anomalous it may appear to many today, it should be remembered that students of the history of political thought ascribe the early theories of popular sovereignty to the canonists, the strong defenders of the papacy. Kingship comes from the people and is responsible to them is the burden of their message. The history of religion in the western world might have been a great deal different had they not so fought. The theory of two separate spheres, the predominance of the spiritual, even in its more correct aspects, the theory of the separation of Church and state—all characteristic of western Christianity—in origin stem from the struggle of the middle ages. Whatever social and religious causes split Christianity asunder in the sixteenth century, the theories of the popes on the independence of the spiritual power was not one of them. Calvin, with all the depth of conviction that led him on, emphasized the independence and superiority of the spiritual with an emphasis that would have astonished Boniface VIII.

Viewing the struggle between the spiritual and the temporal powers in the Middle Ages, Professor Ebenstein sagely remarks: ". . . the papal apologists in seeking to curb the authoritarian claims of kings and princes, or to gain at least equal authority for the church, were (knowingly or unknowingly) fighting a cause that was larger than their own: the whole issue of human liberty was at stake, and it was a more important issue than the rivalry for power and supremacy that rages between popes and emperors . . . The medievalists did not solve this issue, neither have the secularists: Is the state, even the democratic state, to have absolute and complete authority, or must there be some competing principles of allegiance that will make it difficult, or impossible, for the state to become an all-absorbing Leviathan? The church can no longer, as in the Middle Ages, play the part of a competing major source of loyalty and authority, but thus far no institution or idea is in sight that can be relied on to do the job. The democratic state—precisely because of its popular support—has by no means abolished the possibility of tyranny and repression, as was so prophetically foreseen by Alex de Tocqueville and John Stuart Mill a century ago."[43]

Our own times may have been given different insights into this age-old problem, but the problem still remains. Politics and ethics, the latter the concern of the church and state, are not neatly divided. Two schools of thought may be distinguished, to the one belong the hostile and indifferent to religion, to the other belong good religious people for whom God, the Creator of all mankind, exists and must be served. The problem is complicated in our day by the unfortunate division of the latter school, some elements of which readily make friends with the former school to overcome those believers who hold different views on the role of religion in the modern state. By an inexorable rule of politics, this type of unholy alliance will inevitably result in a

---

[43] William Ebenstein, *Great Political Thinkers,* (New York, Rhinehart and Co., 1951).

victory for the enemies of all religion and the creation of a completely secular society. It conceals as many dangers for religious people as the unfortunate alliance of the past between throne and altar.

So long as religion remains, the problem remains. As Foster puts it: "In the 'dirty business of politics' the Christian man will mix by very reason of the grime, because God came to earth to cleanse men. (The author wishes it understood that he does not believe that politics is necessarily a dirty game. The state after all is God's means towards men's temporal, and in an indirect way spiritual end. And politics is necessary for the governance of a state.) In the supreme paradox of the Word Made Flesh is the inspiration to continue the debate. He who is the Church did not deny Caesar and we may not reject our difficulties without denying Christ. The Church will foster and respect the State so long as it is true to its own nature, which is to permit man's growth to his full stature; but it is a stature proportioned to the completed growth of Christ, and to that mystery the Church, and not the State, has the key. On that plane the debate will doubtless continue to the end of time."[44]

[44] Foster, *op. cit.*, pp. 107-8.

CHAPTER II

The Development of American Theory and Practice

In breaking with Rome Henry VIII retained most of the forms of the Catholic Church. His persecution, however, of those who refused to take the Oath of Supremacy, recognizing him as Supreme head of the Church in England, was relentless. Also Condemned were those who brought into England the doctrines of the Reformers—Calvinists or Lutherans. Nevertheless his two able advisers, Thomas Cranmer and Thomas Cromwell, were definitely infected by the new doctrines. Strong resistance to Henry's new order came from a large section of the English people who held firmly to the old faith. On the other hand a sizable part of the population favored the doctrines of the Reformers and were determined that all vestiges of Catholicism should be eliminated. It is the latter group as it developed throughout the years that supplied America with its early settlers.

The young King Edward VI under the direction of his trusted advisers, the Protector Somerset and the Duke of Northumberland, carried the English Church further from its Catholic moorings toward Calvinism. Mary's attempt to restore the Catholic faith in England met with only brief success. In her five-year reign adherents of the Reformed doctrines met with violent suppression or fled to the Continent only to be further indoctrined in the teachings of the Reformation. Their return to England upon the accession of Elizabeth provided Protestantism with a firm and unrelenting group of teachers and leaders who took refuge in the universities, the Inns of Court, and the homes of aristocrats. The settlement under Elizabeth was far from their liking. Her determination to steer a middle course " between

Rome and Geneva" meant the retention of the episcopacy, certain ritualistic practices of the Catholic Church, the belief in a visible Church, other sources than Scripture as the basis of faith, retention of certain feast days and other traditional beliefs and practices. Richard Hooker, otherwise referred to as "the judicious," gave the Elizabethan establishment its philosophy and Hooker borrowed liberally from St. Thomas Aquinas. To the Calvinist group this made the established Church of England no better than Rome; they objected to this watered-down form of Catholicism.

Elizabeth required an Oath of Supremacy to herself as head of the Church and was of no mind to tolerate deviations from what had been established. On the one hand she persecuted the remaining Catholics and on the other the rebellious leaders of the Calvinists. The Calvinists, however, remained within the Church of England and many of them as ministers within that church covertly and sometimes openly spread their teachings and doctrines among their congregations. Most of them had no qualms about taking the Oath of Supremacy. The position of the Catholics was different; they found it impossible to take the Oath of Supremacy, and after the excommunication of Elizabeth, they were definitely regarded as traitors to the realm.

The Calvinist group, however, increased despite the opposition from the throne, and because of their insistence upon "purifying" the established Church in ritual and doctrine became known as Puritans. In general how best describe the Puritan? Professor Simpson puts it this way; "The essence of Puritanism . . . is an experience of conversion which separates the Puritan from the mass of mankind and endows him with privileges and duties of the elect. The root of the matter is always a new birth, which brings with it a conviction of salvation and a dedication to war against sin."[1] His concept of the majesty and sovereignty of God was terrifying to many in his own time and even to his descendants of the present day. All ideas of mercy appear to be removed from the concept, and by a stern predestination God chose his elect and damned the remainder of mankind for His glory. Man knows of his election through a personal experience, a vivid

---

[1] Alan Simpson, *Puritanism in Old and New England* (Chicago: The University of Chicago Press, 1955), p. 2.

experience, following which he is a chosen person and a "Saint." From this point on he needs neither church nor government to light his spiritual course. The Scriptures alone, as he reads them, furnish the guiding teachings. His life, however, must be formed by a rigid self-discipline as severe as any Stoic ever attempted. His church was a bare meeting-house, stripped of all ornamentation, with the pulpit occupying the central position from which the word of God was preached sternly and emphatically in sermons of great length. The world at large was depraved, calling for the regenerating gospel which he was ever ready to preach. In his eyes amusements, merry-making, dancing, the theater, and all the frivolous joys of life were abominations in the sight of the Lord. How could most men be lighthearted when they knew not whether God had damned them to eternal perdition? Not all who bore the name Puritan or who belonged to its numerous sects could live by such an austere code. But the few who did so live provided an indomitable leadership of self-righteous saints who in time shook the very foundations of the English political regime. Armed with a stern code of living, these people faced all the hardships and rigors of settlement in a new world. Passing failure and defeat were but temporary setbacks which no man could avoid, considering his deep sinfulness in the eyes of God. The saint, the converted, the regenerated could shoulder them in the safe assurance of ultimate salvation with all the elect.

What brought him to these shores and what kind of community did he establish? The first Puritans in England, it should be recalled, desired to reform the state church—especially to rid it of episcopacy and ritual. They had no intention of setting up a regime of separation of the temporal from the spiritual or establishing a regime of general religious tolerance. Such a political arrangement entered the minds of few people in the sixteenth century. While the strong elements of individualism indicated in the belief of personal conversion might have resulted in a leaning towards anarchy—as with the Anabaptists on the Continent—organization under strong leadership held the Puritan group together. They were Presbyterians dedicated to the idea of aristocratic government of the elect few in church affairs. They had no opposition to monarchy and aristocracy in civil affairs. Their ideal appeared to be the strong theocratic setup in Geneva or the similar arrangement in Scotland.

Their persecution under Elizabeth was not lessened under James I, who had enough trouble with them when he reigned in Scotland. Their growth in numbers, however, under James' successor, Charles I, brought down upon them severe persecutions engineered through the untiring efforts of Archbishop Laud. They became easy targets, owing to their somber dress and bearing, for the mobs in the cities. Among the new class of gentry and businessmen where they found ever-increasing adherents, they taught the material values of thrift and hard work which brought success to England's middle class. Along with this economic success went the political success of increasing strength in the House of Commons, where the basis of suffrage and election rested upon property qualifications. Charles I's free-wheeling taxing policies were bound to hit the propertied classes most.

This resulted in common political action among a group which had taught the importance of individualism in religious experience. The strife between Parliament and Crown moved from strong but peaceful opposition to civil disturbance, to revolution and regicide, to army control and, finally, Cromwellian dictatorship. In all this disturbance the individualism of the Puritans began to show itself. The Presbyterian group in their religious teachings believed that while the saints should control and teach the church, the unregenerate could be received within it with the lasting hope that they might be converted. The world indeed was evil and sinful—and no people ever had a greater conviction of sin—but the church was in the world and had to find some accommodation to it. They believed that a co-operating government dominated by the saints was the best for this imperfect world. In the dispute with the monarchy they were the conservatives, desiring only that the monarchy "be converted and live." Being people of property, they abhorred violence.

A center group, however, had developed among them, the Congregationalists, who believed that the saints should gather in their own independent houses of worship apart from the unregenerate world. Among many of these the apocalyptic belief was held that in God's good time the righteous would inherit the earth and a regime of the saints would be established. In the meantime the world and its civil governments were judged and were condemned. The political order stood convicted of corruption and was an abomination in the sight of the Lord. Obviously such a group would desire no traffic with civil government. They demanded "soul freedom" with no taint of political control in their religious affairs. They demanded not only separation of church from state, but separation of church from the world. On political forms of regime they had no distinct theories, except for the time of the millennium when the saints would rule. They thought that such a time would have come when the monarchy was gone and Parliament was purged of Anglicans and Presbyterians.

The third group of Puritans, known as the Levellers, formed the backbone of Cromwell's army. These were generally the landless, the propertyless men from the farms and the cities who saw in the Revolution not only a holy crusade but a means of vengeance upon the monarchy, the nobility, and the class-conscious gentry. While mystics were found among the second group, this group contained the larger number. From them came most of the proclamations for a democratic or a republican order of political society—a regime of equality was their aim. Of them Professor Simpson says:

"The Levellers programs, when examined by any disenchanted eye, must have seemed fatuous to the last degree. The idea that a profoundly hierarchical society could be turned into some equalitarian utopia was almost as grotesque an aberration as the idea that the second coming was at hand. He also quickly became objectionable to Puritans who might be enchanted in other ways but not in this way; to Independents like Cromwell and Ireton, who saw that this sort of appeal to natural rights could dissolve the whole social order; or to Milton when he remembered that the mass of the people were an unregenerate rabble. But if the Leveller's moment in history was brief, he made the most of it. He caught up the resentments and aspirations of a lot of little people, dramatized himself and them, and opened a wonderful door of hope as the reward for all strivings. He did this to such effect in the ranks of the revolutionary army that for a time he turned the high command into a debating society where Levellers sat down with the commanding officers to discuss the rights of man. There came a day when the hard-pressed Cromwell thumped the tables as he sat among his officers and cried: 'I tell you, sir, you have no other way to deal with these men but to break them, or they will break you.' And broken they were."[2]

They had their brief day of influence and rule, a tyrannical rule that reached into the avenues of intimate living of men. A somber rule devoid of all humor. A rule that carried unspeakable cruelties beyond the realm of England to the hapless Irish. A rule that before the age of Rousseau set itself the task of compelling men to be free—according to the set pattern of the rulers. As Macaulay put it:

"To the stern precision, even the innocent sport of the fancy seemed a crime. To light and festive natures the solemnity of the zealous brethren furnished copious matter of ridicule. From the Reformation to the civil war, almost every writer, gifted with a fine sense of the ludicrous, had taken some opportunity of assailing the straight-haired, sniffling, whining saints, who christened their children out of the Book of Nehemiah, who groaned in spirit at the sight of Jack in the Green and who thought it impious to taste plum porridge on Christmas Day. At length a time came when the laughers began to look grave in their turn. The rigid ungainly zealots after having furnished much good sport during two generations, rose up in arms, conquered, ruled, and grimly smiling, trod down under their feet the whole crowd of mockers."[3]

On the whole a more sympathetic authority, Professor Perry says of the Puritans:

"He believed himself to be one of the elect, and that implied a moral eminence which contemporaries or later historians have not always found him to occupy. There seems to be a discrepancy between what he was and what he claimed to be. But so it seemed to him also, and hence the perpetual reproach and haunting doubts which beset him. The puritan believed himself to be called, but since his election implied an unnatural and unusual state of godliness, he could not always feel sure of himself. He alternated between the 'very Top of Felicity' and the

---

[2] Alan Simpson, *op. cit.*, pp. 74-75.
[3] Robert Macaulay, *The History of England from the Accession of James II*, Vol. 1, pp. 307-8.

lowest depths of moral despair. It was a life of mountains and valleys with great and precipitous differences of altitude."[4]

The rule of the saints came to an end, with the enthusiastic approval of most of the English people, with the restoration of the monarchy under Charles II. The Anglican worship was now restored and in 1662 and again 1665 Parliament imposed the most severe penalties for any departure from the uses and practices of the Anglican church. The universal theory held by most governments at the time was proclaimed by the king that "nothing conduced more to the settling of the peace of this nation ... than an universal agreement in the public worship of almighty God." This peace, however, was secured by driving thousands of earnest souls into prison or exile. The period, therefore, from the accession of James I in 1603 to the departure of the last Stuart king in 1688 is the period of the great exodus of dissenters to the New World.

Although the dissenters were fleeing from religious persecution at home, would a separation of the temporal and spiritual realms in government and a guarantee of religious toleration characterize the Puritan colonies in New England? Professor Perry gives the answer:

"Puritanism tended to theocracy. It was intolerant of other creeds—in this resembling its God, who might be merciful, but was not tolerant. It was disposed to make its own creed all-pervasive; and to perfect after the scriptural model, all the aspects and social relationships of a life. To achieve this end it did not scruple to employ the full force of the civil authorities, to limit citizenship to members of the church, and to identify its religious ideal with public policy. It enjoyed an invincible sense of truth and felt no compunction in saving unwilling men from the effects of their own blindness. The master motive was the desire to be pure, thorough, strict, and sound—cost what it might."[5]

The Pilgrims who migrated to New England in 1620 were Congregationalists, or Separatists, who had separated from the Anglican church and who believed in the creation of independent,

[4] Ralph Barton Perry, *Puritanism and Democracy* (New York: Vanguard Press, 1944), p. 260.
[5] Ralph Barton Perry, *op. cit.*, p. 115.

self-governing church units. The much larger colony, Massachusetts Bay, settled in 1630 was composed of those Puritans who had not separated from the Anglican church but who entertained the hope of reforming that church along Calvinistic lines. After years of separation from the Anglican establishment they came to follow more closely the Congregationalist model.

These settlers entertained one vision—the setting up of a holy, convenanted community. Believing that properly informed consciences could not disagree on the Word of God, uniformity in belief was to be expected and enforced. Church membership would be confined to the "visible saints," and to the converted and regenerate. Each congregation could find and know the word of God and no disunity could be expected. What of civil authority? "But in a convenanted community the discipline of the state must also be directed by saints. It is true that all Puritans talk about the separation of church and state, and this is one of the things that distinguishes them all from Anglicans. But nine out of ten Puritans only want to separate church and state in order to bind them together again. In other words they have to break the indissoluble unity of church and state in Anglican England so as to get the church on its scriptural basis, Presbyterian or Congregational, as the case may be; but once on that basis, they expect the state to uphold it, to be 'the nursing father' of the church. Separation of church and state, in such context, meant simply a division of functions between two partners with a tendency to reduce the state to a junior partner where the clergy claimed a superior insight in the Divine Will. In New England it was to be expected to be a partnership in unison, for church and state alike were to be dominated by saints."[6]

So the civil authority was to be a council of the saints chosen by the saints, and guided in its deliberations by the preachers of the Word. The people of the new colonies, therefore, were to have an old aristocracy for their government. Any thought of popular government in the modern sense was anathema, and democracy was the meanest and lowest form of government.

But Christianity is not congenial to rigid uniformity. It always

[6] Alan Simpson, *op. cit.*, pp. 25-26.

involves a wide sphere of self-determination. In the last analysis, whatever its form, Christianity teaches the responsibility of each soul before God. It has within it the seeds of rebellion against dominating civil or religious tyranny. Above all, its adherents become most restive when told that any group have a special divine commission to govern the civil affairs of men. On this account Puritan Christianity bred its own form of anticlericalism.

The possibility for the dissenter in early New England of settling elsewhere presented a significant challenge to the dominant authority.

The colonies grew in numbers, however, and people who could lay no claim to spiritual conversion or sainthood made their homes in the midst of the theocrats. As the years go on the preachers declaim against the ungodliness and the lack of discipline existing even in the church itself. The earlier requirements for church membership of divine election through a special mystical experience give way to membership of the children of the elect and finally to all who could subscribe to a creed. An older generation may with Governor Bradford "find and feel the decay" which characterized the new generation, but while state affairs were still firmly bound to church membership, the old severe disciplines had, of necessity, been relaxed.

How a church-state polity could have remained united for any time in enforced unity along with an underlying spirit of individualism is a matter that can only be explained by the acceptance of certain fundamentals of faith and the common trials and dangers in the wilderness which made unity of action and purpose a grave necessity. Any person might at any time claim that he had received a special commission from Providence to proclaim a new gospel. And who could gainsay him? Note the special revelation that came to Master Fawcett, Minister of Walton upon Thames in Surrey. He had a vision and a command from God indicating the following:

"1. That the Sabbath was abolished as unnecessary, Jewish, and merely ceremonial.

2. Tythes are abolished as Jewish and ceremonial, a great burden to the saints of God, and a discouragement of industry.

3. Ministers are abolished as anti-Christian, and of no longer use now Christ himself descends into the hearts of his saints.

4. Magistrates are abolished as useless, now that Christ himself has come amongst us, and hath erected the kingdom of the Saints upon earth.

5. (Pointing to the Bible) Here is a book you have in great veneration . . . I must tell you it is abolished: It containeth beggard rudiments, milk for Babes. . . ."[7]

Despite this heritage of individualism, William Ames could write in colonial New England: "If therefore Heretikes be manifestly known and publicly hurtfull, they are to be restrained of the Magistrates by publike power. And if they be manifestly blasphemous, and pertenacious, and stubborne in those blasphemies may suffer capitall punishment."[8] Perhaps this is something of the spirit which led Voltaire to say: "If there had been in England only one religion, its despotism would have been fearful. If there had been two religions, they would have cut each other's throats. But as there are thirty, they live peacefully and happily."[9]

In any case dissent did arise and resulted in the forced exile of the dissenters and the founding of further settlements. Roger Williams landed at Boston in 1631. He early showed his independence by refusing to join the congregation of the Boston church because it had not separated completely from the Anglican church. The congregation at Salem invited him to be its minister but the General Court (legislature) of Massachusetts vetoed this plan. After spending a couple of years as a minister in Plymouth he returned to the Salem church where for two years he expounded his views, which to John Cotten and others were dangerous to the public weal. He was brought to trial and condemned on the following charges:

"First, that we have not our land by patent from the king, but that the natives are the true owners of it, and that we ought to repent of such receiving it by patent.

"Secondly, That it is not lawful to call a wicked person to swear, (or) pray, as being actions of God's worship.

[7] Quoted in Alan Simpson, *op. cit.*, pp. 54-55, from *Anarchia Anglicans, Or History of Independence* (London, 1649) Part II, pp. 152-53.
[8] Quoted from Loren Beth, *The American Theory of Church and State* (Gainesville, Florida: University of Florida Press, 1958), p. 36.
[9] Voltaire, *Lettres Philosophiques*, Ed. G. Lanson (Paris: Societe Nouvelle di Librairie et d'Edition, 1909), I, 74.

"Thirdly, That it is not lawful to hear any of the ministers of of the Parish assemblies in England.

"Fourthly, That the civil magistrate's power extends only to bodies, and goods, and outward state of men."[10]

The last charge containing the theory of separation of church and state formed part of the teachings of the Congregationalists and Separatists in England but was not particularly welcomed by most of this group in America. Exiled from Massachusetts, Williams made his way to the present site of Providence in Rhode Island. Here he desired to found a settlement "for persons distressed for conscience" and founded on the basis of a covenant in which all would abide by the will of the majority but "only in civil things." His ideas of the relation of the temporal and spiritual is stated in his *The Boudy Tenent of Persecution* (Vol. III, p. 76):

> (1) *God* requireth not an *uniformity* of *Religions* to be *inacted* and *inforced* in any *civill state;* which inforced *uniformity* (sooner or later) is the greatest occasion of *civill Warre, ravishing of conscience, persecution* of *Jesus Christ,* in his servants, and of the *hypocrisie* and destruction of millions of souls. (2) It is the will and command of God, that . . . a *permission* of the most *Paganish, Jewish, Turkis,* or *Anti-Christian consciences* and worships, bee granted to *all* men in all *Nations* and *Countries:* and they are only to be fought against with *Sword* which is only (in *Souls matter*) *able* to *conquer,* to wit, *the Sword of God's Spirit,* the *Word of God.* (3) True *civility* and *Christianity* may both flourish in a *state* or *Kingdome,* nothwithstanding the *permission* of divers and contrary consciences, either Jew or *Gentile.*"

This was a bold proposition for the time. Few believed that a free conscience in a spiritual sense could at the same time be bound in a social or political sense. And it was true that some of the more zealous reformers had been teaching that civil government, being an evil, could not be submitted to. This was the anarchic doctrine of which the Anabaptists had been accused. Williams, on the other hand, was a believer in the contract theory of government frequently found in the writings of political theorists of the seventeenth century. The main tenets of this

[10] Quoted in William Sweet, *The Story of Religions in America* (New York: Harper & Brothers, 1930), p. 100.

were that civil society comes into being by an agreement among free men and that civil obligations are assumed by that agreement. If the government set up by this process breaks the agreement by oppression or lawlessness, citizens are free to rebel or to set up another government. The contract theory was generally held by the leaders of the American Revolution and the founders of the Republic.

To Rhode Island went another exile from Massachusetts, Anne Hutchinson. She was accused of false doctrines by Reverend John Wilson and condemned in the following language.

"Forasmuch as you, Mrs. Hutchinson, have highly transgressed and offended and forasmuch as you have so many ways troubled the church with your errors and have drawn away many a poor soul, and have upheld your revelations; . . . Therefore in the name of our Lord Jesus Christ and in the name of the church I do not only pronounce you worthy to be cast out, but I do cast you out and in the name of Christ I do deliver you up to Satan. . . ." So also John Clark, Samuel Gorton, William Coddington sought refuge from the severity of the laws—ecclesiastical and civil—in Rhode Island. This group would have affirmed Williams's three propositions as stated by Professor Simpson.

"First, that forced worship stinks in God's nostrils; second, that forced worship denies the coming of Christ by insisting on the national church of the Jews; third, that religious liberty is the only prudent way of preserving peace in the world."[11] So the church becomes a voluntary association in a secularized state and all churches have the same liberty. Williams made no exception in his toleration of Catholics for they too were to be granted freedom, albeit in Williams' day there were no Catholics in Rhode Island. After the Revolution of 1688 in England, when the Catholic James II was driven out and the Toleration Act of 1689 deprived English Catholics of civil and religious rights, a phrase depriving Catholics of their rights was interpolated in the Rhode Island Charter. It was not removed by the Rhode Island legislature until 1783.

In another early colony to the south, Virginia, there were inroads by Presbyterians and dissenters, but the colony remained

[11] Alan Simpson, *op. cit.*, p. 48.

Anglican by law. The establishment, however, was weak. The population was scattered over large areas on plantations. The distance between churches was great. It was not only difficult to support churches and ministers but difficult to maintain a closely-built organization of the whole church. Unlike the Congregational ministers in New England, the Anglican ministers in Virginia were subject to a distant authority, the Bishop of London. The laxity of living among some of them brought frequent complaints from the colonists and disrespect for the church. Unlike New England the state control of the church in Virginia was more definitely pronounced. While theoretically toleration extended only to Anglicans, other dissenting groups came to be accepted when they grew strong and respectable enough. This toleration did not, however, extend to Baptists and Catholics. The Baptists with their strong conviction on separation of church and state were persecuted down to the Revolution. The English Toleration Act of 1689, which excluded the Catholics from toleration, was enforced in Virginia until the Revolution.

Cecil Calvert, second Lord Baltimore, was by terms of the charter "Absolute Lord of Maryland and Avalon." As proprietor of the colony his power of Lordship was subject to the English king alone. He was head of both church and state. The charter of the proprietary grant provided only for the maintenance of "God's holy and true Christian religion." The area covered by the charter already had a sizable number of Protestants in it when the brother of Cecil Calvert, Leonard, came to take it over. The instructions given by Cecil Calvert to his brother (1633) on the regulations to be observed on board ship bringing the colonists are interesting. He admonishes him, since Protestants were among them, that all religious acts of the Catholics be done as privately as possible, that Catholics should not enter any religious disputes with Protestants, and that the acts of Catholics in no way give scandal or offense to the Protestants. In 1649 the legislative assembly of the colony, composed of both Catholics and Protestants, passed with the approval of the governor a toleration act providing religious freedom for all "professing to believe in Jesus Christ" and who accepted his divinity. The doctrine of the Trinity had to be accepted. The punishment for the denial of the Trinity was death or confiscation of lands—

penalities not unusual in the colonies. The same act provided that anyone who used the following terms in a reproachful manner would be fined ten shillings or publicly whipped—"heretik, Schismatick, Idolator, Puritan, Independent, Prespiterian, popish priest, Jesuite, Jesuited papist, Lutheran, Calvinist, Anabaptist, Brownist, Antinomian, Barrowist, Roundhead, Separatist." Obviously the key word in the act is "reproachful" for some of these terms had already become respectable.

During the period of Puritan ascendancy in England the Lord Proprietor was deprived of his colony and an "Act Concerning Religions" was passed providing that all who accepted the Trinity would enjoy toleration and civic rights but that "none who profess and exercise the Popish religion, commonly known by the name of the Roman Catholic religion, can be protected in this province . . . and are to be restrained from the exercise thereof." In 1658 Lord Baltimore was once more given care of the colony and the Toleration Act of 1649 was gain put in force.

After the Revolution of 1688 in England the Calverts were once again deprived of their colony, which became a royal colony with the Church of England established. Once again the Catholics were deprived of protection, toleration, and the right to worship. The Protestants had become a majority, but they increasingly feared Catholic immigration, especially from Ireland, and every effort was put forth to restrict the freedom of Catholics. The colony was restored to the Calverts in 1715 under the fifth Lord Baltimore, who had become a Protestant, but the lot of the Catholics was in no wise improved. As Professor Sweet says: "This has been termed one of the sarcasms of history. Maryland, which had been founded for the sake of religious freedom by the toil and treasure of Roman Catholics, was now open to all who call themselves Christian save Roman Catholics."[12]

In lieu of £16,000 which the Crown owed to his family, William Penn, Quaker, was given a proprietary grant over what is now Pennsylvania and Delaware. Like the Separatists, the Quakers were firm believers in the separation of the temporal and the spiritual. Civil government, they taught, should maintain peace but should not interfere in matters of conscience. In his

[12] William Sweet, *op. cit.*, p. 64.

"Frame of Government" published in 1682, Penn provided that "All persons who profess to believe in Jesus Christ, the Saviour of the World, shall be capable to serve this government in any capacity, both legislatively and executively." Thus Protestants and Catholics alike were eligible for public office. While only Christians could hold office, general toleration was extended to others by the following: "That no person, now, or at any time hereafter, Living in this Province, who shall confess and acknowledge one Almighty God to be the Creator, Upholder and Ruler of the world, And who professes, him or herself obliged in conscience to live peaceably and quietly under the civil government, shall in any case be molested or prejudiced for his, or her conscientious persuasion or practice. . . . And if any persons shall abuse or deride any other, for his, or her different persuasion or practice in matters of religion, such person shall be lookt upon as a disturber of the peace, and be punished accordingly."[13] While later Penn was forced by the English government to apply the Test Act and thus deprive the Catholics of the right to hold office, the general principles of toleration remained. The results of the policy were evident by the time of the Revolution; as Professor Stokes points out, there were 403 different congregations in Pennsylvania. Of these, 106 were German Reformed, 68 were Presbyterian, 63 were Lutheran, 61 were Quakers, 33 were Episcopalian, 27 were Baptist, 14 were Moravian, 13 were Mennonites, 13 were German Baptist Brethren, 9 were Catholics, and 1 was Dutch Reformed.

In 1621 The Dutch West India Company was granted a charter by the Netherlands government to trade and found colonies in America. Shortly thereafter thirty Dutch and Walloon Protestants came to America, one group settling near the present site of Camden, New Jersey, and the other at the present site of Albany, then named Fort Orange. By the time of the arrival of the first Dutch governor, Peter Minuit, in 1625, there were about two hundred colonists. It was Minuit who purchased Manhattan Island from the Indians and who built a settlement at the southern tip of the Island. While the Dutch in coming to these shores were mainly interested in the pursuit of trade, the Dutch West

[13] Charter to William Penn, and Laws of the Province of Pennsylvania, Passed between the Years 1682 and 1700 (Harrisburg, 1879), pp. 107-8.

India Company declared the Reformed religion established and provided the necessary means of living for ministers and teachers of that faith. Among the more famous of the Dutch ministers brought over from Holland by Killian Van Rensselaer, was John Van Mekelenburg, known as Megapolensis.

Megapolensis was the local minister at Rensselaerwyck when Father Jogues, the French Jesuit missionary, escaping from the wrath of the Iroquois Indians, sought refuge in Albany. Father Jogues was shown marked hospitality by the Dutch governor and Megapolensis and given safe conduct to New Amsterdam. Professor Sweet quotes Father Jogues' description of New Amsterdam at that time: "No religion is publicly exercised but the Calvinist, the orders are to admit none but Calvinist. But this is not observed, for there are, besides Calvinists, in the colony, Catholics, English, Puritans, Lutherans, Anabaptists—here called Mennonites."[14]

The last of the Dutch governors, Peter Stuyvesant, evidently held firm ideas on the necessity for church establishment, but he was called to task for the severity of his persecution by the Dutch West India Company, who declared that they believed, "that some connivance would be useful." Persecution was bad business practice.

When the English took over the colony in 1664, Charles II made his brother, the Catholic Duke of York (later James II), proprietor. The English governor continued to support the Dutch ministers. "The best of all the early English governors of New York," declares Professor Sweet, "was the Irish Roman Catholic Governor Dongan (1682–1688). He was an honest and broad-minded man and on his arrival announced to the Dutch minister at New York, upon whom he called, that the Duke intended to allow liberty of conscience. . . . It has been stated, with justice, that religious toleration was almost perfect during the administration of Dongan, though the instructions were sent to the governor by James II, who was we will remember himself a Catholic, establishing the Church of England in the colony." Sweet notes the following instruction sent by James to the governor: "You shall permit all persons of what Religion soever

[14] William Sweet, *op. cit.*, p. 128.

quietly to inhabit within your government without giving them any disturbance or disquiet whatsoever for or by reason of their differing opinions in matters of Religion, Provided they give no disturbance to ye public peace, nor do molest or disquiet others in ye free exercise of their religion."[15]

But the old story was repeated in New York as it had been elewhere. When James II was driven out and the Protestants William and Mary ascended the throne, the new governor declared liberty of conscience for all *except papists*. All office holders had to take the oath of allegiance to the supremacy of the monarchy, to receive the sacrament according to the form of the Church of England, and to sign a declaration against the Catholic doctrine of transubstantiation. In addition public support was supplied for the Church of England ministers. The influx of many immigrants into New York brought about a practical tolerance despite the restrictions for holding office.

While the colony of New Jersey provided that "no person shall ever, within this colony, be deprived of the inestimable privilege of worshipping Almighty God in a manner agreeable to the dictates of his conscience," it further provided "that no Protestant inhabitant of this Colony shall be denied the enjoyment of any civil right and . . . all persons . . . professing a belief in the faith of any Protestant sect . . . shall be capable of being elected into any office of profit or trust. . . ." It was not until 1844 that Catholics were permitted to vote in New Jersey and the restrictions on office holding was not withdrawn until many years later.

The situation in the colonies before the Revolution may be summarized as follows:

1. All colonies except Rhode Island had laws unfavorable in one way or another to Catholics and Jews.

2. New Jersey, Pennsylvania, and Delaware had no established church. The latter two were tolerant insofar as the laws of England allowed.

3. Massachusetts, Connecticut and New Hampshire had Congregational establishments.

4. Maryland, Virginia, the Carolinas, Georgia, and, rather tenuously, New York had Anglican church establishments.[16]

---

[15] William Sweet, *op. cit.*, pp. 133-34.
[16] See Loren Beth, *op. cit.*, pp. 59-60.

This situation played a great part in preventing the people of Quebec from joining the American colonies in the war of the Revolution, although strenuous efforts by the Carrolls of Maryland and others to persuade them to join in the struggle were made.

While there had been a great religious awakening in the colonies in the mid-eighteenth century led by such men as Theodorus Frelinghuysen, Jonathan Edwards, George Whitefield, and others, religious fervor at the time of the Revolution and immediately thereafter sunk to a low ebb. The awakening itself is said to have had certain democratizing effects. Professor Gewehr says: "If a study of the rise of dissent in the XVIII century shows anything, it is the fact that the Great Awakening was one the secret springs which directed the actions of men, and, therefore, was one of the sources of the democratic movement so closely identified with the American Revolution. . . . The Great Awakening gave rise to popular forms of Church government and thus accustomed people to self-government in their religious habits. The alliance of Church and State, the identification of religious with civil institutions, was found to be detrimental to the cause of religion. . . . Perhaps unconsciously, but none the less in reality, the Great Awakening gradually welded the common people into a democracy which in the end was to change inevitably the temper, if not the form, of government. . . ."[17] At the time of the revolution, although there were about three million people (one-sixth were slaves) in the colonies and over three thousand congregations of various groups, only about thirty-five per cent of the people were church members. The great mobility of the population, the settlement of large numbers on the frontier where churches were nonexistent, the general economic and political upheaval, and the inroads of the ideas of the Enlightenment all played a part in the weakening of religious faith. The early Americans were still fundamentally a religious people even if many were not church members, but attachment to specific creeds had lessened.

Political ideas were undoubtedly influenced by many of the leaders of the Revolution who were Deists. These people accepted

[17] Wesley M. Gewehr, *The Great Awakening in Virginia* (Durham, N.C.: Duke University Press, 1930), p. 187.

a belief in a Divine Being, the God of nature, but with strong emphasis on nature. God had created the world once and for all and at that point had disappeared into a shadowy realm. The world had been set going, wound up like a clock, and henceforth was to proceed on its own momentum, with plants, animals, and men pursuing their own courses according to nature. Newtonian physics had played a prominent role in these beliefs, and the political philosophy of John Locke in its special emphasis on natural rights did not contradict the prevailing opinions. A strong strain of individualism underlay this belief—individualism in religious belief, individualism in politics, and individualism in economics. Government was necessary, but to many Deists, notably Jefferson, a necessary evil. Religion was a personal affair with which neither society nor government should interfere. A considerable measure of skepticism accompanied religious belief. Despite all this, Deists could affirm a belief in God and respect for religion.

It is difficult to say how much of this thinking affected the masses, but many of the leaders in public life such as Thomas Paine, Thomas Jefferson, George Mason, John Adams, and Benjamin Franklin were either declared Deists or sympathetic to their views. None of the first four presidents, it should be recalled, belonged to any specific church.

This is not to say that the leaders of the churches played no part in the Revolution and the first years of independence. Professor Sweet says of their activity and influence: "No church in the American colonies had so large an influence in bringing on the war for Independence as had the Congregational. Its ministry had been most influential in public affairs from the beginning, and although the political influence of the New England ministers in the eighteenth century was not so great as in the century previous, yet their opinions on all public matters were still of great weight. . . . The Presbyterians in the colonies at the opening of the Revolution were largely Scotch-Irish and represented the most recent immigration, that from Northern Ireland, and were still burning with hostility to England for the wrongs which had caused their migration."[18]

[18] William Sweet, *op. cit.*, pp. 256 and 259.

The ire of many of the Protestant clergy and not a few lay leaders was aroused against England by the passage of the Quebec Act of 1774. Today most people would say that the Act does credit to an overwhelming Protestant government such as existed in England in dealing with its new French subjects in Canada. The scope of the Act included not only Quebec but practically all of the territory covered by the present states of Ohio, Indiana, Illinois, and Wisconsin; the latter territory was ceded to the United States by Britain after the Revolution. The Act provided that the whole region would be governed from Quebec under French civil law and English criminal law and that Catholics should enjoy the free exercise of their religion. It further provided that publicly collected money would be used for the support of the Catholic Church; but government funds could also be used for the encouragement of the Protestant religion. In other words the state would support the churches. In this country, however, these provisions were interpreted as the setting up of an established Catholic Church. This not only aroused the anger of men like Alexander Hamilton, Samuel Adams, and John Adams, but of the Continental Congress itself.

Samuel Adams stated that "much more is to be dreaded from the growth of the popery in America, than from Stamp-Acts or *any other* Acts destructive of men's civil rights."[19] And John Adams protested that "the barriers against popery, erected by our ancestors, are suffered to be destroyed, to the hazard even of the Protestant religion."[20] In October of 1774 the Continental Congress protested the Quebec Act "To the people of Britain" in the following words: "Nor can we suppress our astonishment, that a British Parliament should even consent to establish in that country (Canada) a religion that had deluged your island in blood, and dispersed bigotry, persecution, murder and rebellion through every part of the world."[21]

Professor Stokes says of the Act: "As a result, the Act was a factor of some importance in bringing on disaffection which led to the American Revolution, partly because it seemed to prevent the western expansion of Virginia and other colonies. It was

[19] Writings of Samuel Adams, I, 201.
[20] John Adams, *Works*, II, 252.
[21] *Journal of Continental Congress*, Ford Ed., O I, 117.

considered one of the five 'Intolerable Acts' of Parliament, and was referred to in veiled terms in the Declaration of Independence as one of the many acts of the King having as one object 'the establishment of an absolute Tyranny over the States.'" The Declaration of Independence condemned the King "for abolishing the Free system of English Laws in a neighboring province, establishing therein an Arbitrary government, and enlarging its boundaries so as to render it at once an example and fit instrument for introducing the same absolute rule into these colonies. . . .'"[22] It is on this basis that Professor Claude Van Tyne concludes: "In fact, the whole colonial period must be studied, and many conditions noted . . . before one may at all comprehend why the American people rebelled in 1775. Among the many causes, I rate religious bigotry, sectarian antipathy, and the influence of the Calvinistic clergy . . ."[23] No wonder the people of Quebec did not respond with any enthusiasm when the Americans proposed that they join in the War for Independence!

In the formation of the early state constitutions certain groups stand out in the battle for liberalizing the early fundamental laws: the small group of leaders already mentioned who were influenced by the Enlightenment, the Baptists, the unchurched, and a large number of Presbyterians, particularly in the South.

In Virginia, where the Episcopal church was by law established, the church was endowed with large sections of land, and the clergy were recompensed by salaries fixed by law in pounds of tobacco. Each year a clergyman was supposed to receive eight tons of tobacco. The struggle against the established church began as early as 1758. There had been a shortage in the tobacco crop which brought a great increase in its price. Many vestries of the church complained that they could not meet the fixed salaries at the going market price of tobacco. At this point the Virginia legislature intervened and declared a lower rate than the market rate for the payment of ministers. The Board of Trade in London invalidated the action. From this point forward a number of attempts were made to cut the powers of the estab-

---

[22] Anson Phelps Stokes, *Church and State in the United States* (New York: Harper & Brothers, 1950), pp. 263-64.
[23] Quoted in Anson Phelps Stokes, *op. cit.*, p. 261.

lished church, the Baptists and the Deists generally being in the forefront of the struggle. Such well-known figures of American history as James Madison, Patrick Henry, George Mason, and Thomas Jefferson played notable roles in the struggle. Jefferson stated that it was the "severest contest in which I have ever been engaged." The struggle lasted several years, from 1760 to 1802, when the question of church lands was settled. Within that time, on June 26, 1776, the Virginia Assembly passed the Declaration of Rights drawn up by George Mason. It included the significant paragraph: "That religion, or the duty which we owe to our Creator, and the manner of discharging it, can be directed only by reason and conviction, not by force or violence, and therefore all men are equally entitled to the free exercise of religion, according to the dictates of conscience; and that it is the mutual duty of all to practice Christian forbearance, love, and charity towards each other."[24]

All dissenters from the established church were freed from taxation for its support. Later, dissenting clergymen were given the right to perform the marriage ceremony, a right formerly reserved for Episcopalian clergymen. In October of 1785 Patrick Henry, with a numerous backing from the assembly and with most Protestants in the state, including such men as Edmund Randolph and George Washington, fathered a plan for the support of all Christian clergy by the state. Owing to the indomitable opposition of James Madison and Baptist groups the plan was defeated. Later in the same year Thomas Jefferson's "Bill for Establishing Religious Freedom" was passed by the Virginia Legislature. No church from henceforth was entitled to public support and the whole intent of the bill may be found in one of the concluding paragraphs: "*We, the General Assembly, do enact,* That no man shall be compelled to frequent or support any religious worship, place, or ministry whatsoever, nor shall be enforced, restrained, molested, or burdened in his body or goods nor shall otherwise suffer, on account of his religious opinion or belief; but that all men shall be free to profess, and by argument to maintain, their opinions in matters of religion, and that the same shall in no wise diminish, enlarge, or affect their civil

[24] Quoted from Anson Phelps Stokes, *op cit.*, I, 303.

capacities."[25] Thus Virginia joined Rhode Island in church-state separation.

No struggle for the freedom of religion was more prolonged than in Massachusetts. Not until 1833 was the battle won. As early as 1631 the General Court (legislature) enacted that "to the end that the body of the commons may be presumed of honest and good men, . . . for the time to come shall no man be admitted to the freedom of this body politic but such as are members of some of the churches within the limits of the same."[26] This meant the Congregational churches. In 1638 a tax was levied on all who did not contribute to the support of the local Congregationalist ministry. All had not only to support the ministers but to defray the cost of the building of the Congregational churches. To rid the colony of the Baptists and Quakers, the General Court decreed banishment for all heretics. Despite requests, and orders from the monarchy in England (Charles II and William and Mary) to lift restrictions on other Protestants, the colony went on its traditional way. Before the Revolution, however, Episcopalians, Baptists, and Quakers were permitted to have the publicly collected taxes applied to their own places of worship.

In 1780 Massachusetts adopted a state constitution; a summary of its articles on religion follows:

I "All men are ' orn free and equal, and have certain natural, essential, and unalie. ble rights. . . ."

II "It is the right as well as the duty of all men in society, publicly, and at stated seasons, to worship the Supreme Being, the great Creator and Power of the Universe. And no subject shall be hurt, molested, or restrained, in his person, liberty, or estate, for worshipping God in the manner and season most agreeable to the dictates of his own conscience. . . ."

III "As the happiness of a people, and the good order and preservation of civil government, essentially depend upon piety, religion, and morality . . . the people of this commonwealth have a right to invest their legislature with power to authorize and require . . . the several towns . . . and other bodies politic, or

---

[25] Quoted in Anson Phelps Stokes, *op. cit.*, pp. 393-94.
[26] A. H. Newman, *History of the Baptist Churches in the United States*, (New York: The Christian Literature Co., 1894), p. 63.

religious societies, to make suitable provision, at their own expense, for the instruction of the public worship of God, and for the support and maintenance of public Protestant teachers of piety, religion, and morality, in all cases where such provision shall not be made voluntarily."[27]

The constitution went on to say that if one did not wish to pay taxes for the support of a Congregational minister, the monies collected could be given to his own sect. If he did not belong to any or if his own sect had no church, then the tax would have to go to the Congregational establishment. The legislature was also empowered to compel attendance "upon the instructions of the public teacher" of people who conscientiously could attend. In 1820 changes in these parts of the Constitution were voted down. In 1833 all religious groups were made self-sustaining and Massachusetts finally joined the other states in separating church and state.

The battle for recognition of all religious groups and the elimination of discriminatory clauses in the constitution came about in 1818 in Connecticut. The struggle in this state was intensified by the fact that the Congregationalist group and its leaders were allied with the Federalist Party. A split in the ranks of the Congregationalists along with the fall of the Federalist Party, owing to its active opposition to the War of 1812, brought about a situation propitious for a broadening of the constitutional provision.

In summary it may be said that while conditions varied in the colonies and states, church establishment had a long history and was broken in some states only with the increase of dissenting sects. Catholics (in Maryland and Pennsylvania) and Jews (in New York) were but a handful of the population. They were not numerous enough to affect the situation. The Baptists, some Presbyterians, some dissenting Congregationalists, some Methodists, and the Deists constituted the main and ever-growing strength of the opposition to church establishment and special recognition of any one religious group. Nor must one forget the large number of the unchurched; a growing number of them in the middle states were religious, if at all, only by inheritance.

[27] Constitution of Massachusetts, 1780, Art. XXII, 2.

While the Deists talked in terms of an absolute freedom, even for "Turks" and infidels, it was generally assumed that the foundations of American society were religious. Whatever religious views Thomas Jefferson held, and they are not easy to determine, he found it necessary to defend himself against charges of being an atheist. The gratitude to Almighty God for the blessings of peace and liberty expressed in the new constitutions demonstrated at least that the civil order and the spiritual order had something in common. But one may also say, because fears were experienced that this might not always be true, that the assumption was that American society was Protestant in some form or other. Notice should be taken of this assumption along with the strong nationalistic tendencies among the Protestant groups—tendencies that gave the Protestant leaders a strong feeling that they established this country, that Protestantism in some form or other produced its institutions, and that in general to be American and Protestant were one and the same thing. Even the theory of separation of church and state before long came to be looked upon as a special contribution to American polity by Protestants, although as we have seen many Protestants fought it bitterly. Professor Stokes says that even the early Unitarians in Massachusetts opposed it. The Catholics and their leaders were strong supporters of the separation idea and the letters of the first Catholic bishop, John Carroll, are replete with praise of the American solution which had found its way into most of the state constitutions. In a letter which appeared in 1784 he declared that he would refrain even from a controversial defense of his faith "if I could fear that it would disturb the harmony now subsisting amongst all Christians in this country, so blessed with civil and religious liberty; which, if we have the wisdom and the temper to persevere, America may come to exhibit a proof to the world, that general and equal toleration, by giving a free circulation to fair argument, is the most effectual method to bring all denominations of Christians to a unity of faith."[28]

If the American churches were nationalistic they were also separated from their European counterparts. To the Protestants

---

[28] Quotation from Anson Phelps Stokes, *op. cit.*, I, 327.

of the early days of the Republic (even to Protestants in our day)
the Catholic Church was European, a belief so frequently expressed at the present time that Catholics have been driven into
an overassertion, even an hysterical assertion, of their Ameri-
canism. In the early American history we are considering, the
Catholics, too, had a strong nationalistic outlook, expressed by
Bishop Carroll in his desire for a special arrangement for the
Church in this country such as freedom from as many controls
from Rome as possible, for an American hierarchy, and for the
use of English in place of Latin in the liturgy. In a letter written in
the year 1787 Bishop Carroll wrote: "In a letter to him [the Reverend Joseph Berington] and before I had a thought of ever being
in my present station, I expressed a wish that the pastors of the
Church would see cause to grant to this extensive continent
jointly with England and Ireland, etc. the same privilege as is
enjoyed by many churches of infinitely less extent; that of having
their liturgy in their own language; for I do indeed conceive that
one of the most popular prejudices against us is that our public
prayers are unintelligible to our hearers. Many of the poor
people, and the negroes generally, not being able to read, have
no technical help to confine their attention. . . ."[29]

It is not easy to enter into the minds and the motives of a
people of another age. Yet some assertions may be safely made
about the framers of the Constitution. They knew they were
dealing with thirteen states which regarded themselves as *free*
and *independent* and which were jealous of their special rights.
The framers faced a situation in which some of these states
maintained religious establishments that no central authority
dared tamper with. Yet the members of the Constitutional Convention undoubtedly held the view that as far as the central
authority was concerned, neutrality in matters of religion should
be the established rule. Even the name of God does not appear
in the fundamental law. Although some of the most influential
members of the Convention were Deists, respect for religion in
a general sense was not lacking. One might conclude that the
remarks of the caustic, abrasive Alexander Hamilton on one
occasion indicated a hostile attitude. This was the occasion when

[29] Quoted by Anson Phelps Stokes, *op. cit.*, I, 329.

the Constitutional Convention reached a serious impasse on the problem of representation in the proposed national legislature. The aging Franklin suggested that prayers be offered for Divine guidance. They were not offered after Hamilton objected on the ground that he was opposed to importation of "foreign aid." Let us assume that the remark came as a result of the intense heat of a Philadelphia summer combined with the general irritability and frustration which many members felt at the time.

On matters of religion the members decided to deal with the central government alone and even then with great brevity. Article VI, the wording of which we owe to Charles Pinckney, reads in part: "No religious test shall ever be required as a Qualification to any office of public Trust under the United States." Only North Carolina voted against this clause, but as Professor Stokes points out, some feared even in that time that the pope might one day become president and only Catholics would be admitted to office! Even in the eighteenth century the possibility of the pope's becoming executive of any secular state was dim indeed. Article VI, however, was as far as the delegates were willing to go.

Owing to a demand that the states be further protected from the acts of the central government, the first Congress proposed the first ten amendments, which the states subsequently accepted. The first of these reads: "Congress shall make no law respecting the establishment of religion, or prohibiting the free exercise thereof or abridging the freedom of speech or of the press; or of the right of the people peaceably to assemble and to petition the government for a redress of grievances." On this amendment Professor Stokes comments: "These rights are interrelated. They are all of importance from the standpoint of the Churches. Freedom of speech is related to preaching; freedom of the press to religious journalism; freedom of assembly and petition to Church meetings. . . ."[30]

That the Congress and the people had a more restricted idea of what this amendment meant than many people today is evidenced from the fact that days of Thanksgiving were proclaimed from the very inception of the national government (Jefferson

[30] Anson Phelps Stokes, *op. cit.*, p. 539.

refrained from the practice), that the hall of the House of Representatives was set aside for regular Sunday services (Jefferson attended these with fair regularity), a practice which continued until after the Civil War (The Catholic bishop of Charleston, John England, gave an address at one of these services in 1826 at the invitation of President John Quincy Adams), and that the opening session of Congress always opened with a prayer. If one may hazard a guess it may be said that considering the restriction against Catholics, Jews, and infidels still existing in some state constitutions, the general assumption seemed to exist that America's social background would remain Protestant and that the federal government must in no way show favoritism among the various Protestant sects.

Throughout the nineteenth century only one outstanding case involving the first amendment to the federal Constitution arose. This case involved the practice of polygamy among the Mormons in Utah. On the basis of the necessity of maintenance of law and order, the principles of the common law, and the basic practices in western society, the Supreme Court ruled that Congress could outlaw polygamy in the territories without denying freedom of religion (*Reynolds* v. *U.S.* 98 U.S., 145, 1879). During this period the federal government was a limited government both in theory and practice, although the possibility of the expansion of its powers over the economic life was gradually becoming evident with the application of the commerce clause. The states exercised all residual powers for the general welfare of the citizens. As yet no clause of the federal Constitution was interpreted as barring the states from establishing religion or restricting religious toleration. But the states were moving away from legislation of this nature and by mid-nineteenth century there were adopted restrictive clauses in their Constitutions prohibiting the expenditure of public funds for religious purposes. The growth of the Catholic population in the urban centers of the east and the fear that public funds would be used to finance their schools was largely responsible for the passage of these restrictive provisions. In centers where the Catholic population was growing in number the Protestant groups became more insistent that all religious influence be removed from the public schools.

It should be remembered, however, that a rigid interpretation of the separation of church and state, while growing, was as yet not evident in practice. Laws "making holy the Sabbath Day" existed in all the states and in some were strictly enforced; Bible reading was common in the public schools (King James version); sumptuary legislation on gambling, liquor sales, and even blasphemy was found in many states. All public events opened with prayer. The occasional Catholic or Jew raised to public office not infrequently caused open public hostility.

Nevertheless on the theoretical side Americans boasted of their religious freedom, and in large measure, by the last quarter of the nineteenth century, they had good reason to boast. Catholics, like Cardinal Gibbons, could tell the world that we were a most favored land and that Catholics occupied an enviable position in the freedom they enjoyed. So strong was the defense of the American way by certain Catholic leaders that Rome itself became suspicious of their orthodoxy.

The average American would have said that religion and politics should not be mixed. The more erudite American would have said that the temporal and the spiritual had two different ends to serve and that while there might be a relationship between the two, neither should perform the work of the other. All Americans would have said that history gave some horrible lessons of what happened to church, state, and citizens when the functions of the temporal and spiritual spheres depended too much one upon the other. Since hostility to religion did not figure in the idea of separation in the United States, it would have been contended that the health of the Church itself needed this separation. To most Americans, being a practical people, the pluralistic nature of their society made separation a necessity about which no great amount of theoretical reasoning had to be given.

The twentieth century, however, was to bring new problems in which the relationship of church and state became matters of great political and social concern. The acceptance of the American doctrine by all parties involved in the controversies made neither for more reasoned understanding nor for greater clarification by the institution of last resort—the judiciary. The relation of church and state is not a fixed relationship and undoubtedly each generation has to decide in connection with the problems existent at the time what is the proper sphere of each. The Middle Ages in western Europe, as we have seen, had no easier answer than we have today to the vexed problems and often met them with greater violence. All this despite the fact that Europe was unified under one faith. The variety of relationships between church and state found throughout the world today indicates the various answers that are given to the problem, and the answers arise from social experience, history, and the genius of a people. The great danger arising here, as elsewhere, is a too rigid and doctrinaire interpretation of a basic theory objectively true but—in a society of human beings, as distinct from angels—subjectively applied.

CHAPTER III

Church and State Theory

What are the Catholic theories on church and state? At the outset, it should be pointed out as obvious that no Catholic could accept the union of church and state which would blur the distinction between the two. The Catholic also rejects the principle of modern positivism that makes every act of the state legal because it is enacted by the state—a doctrine that sets aside divine or natural law as a standard by which all political acts must be measured. The Catholic also refuses to accept any idea of separation of church and state which sets off each in an isolated compartment, each part having no relationship in co-operating for the common good. The Church cannot ignore men's temporal needs. The Church has a vital concern in whether a man receives a living wage, whether he lives in decent housing, whether his treatment is fair, humane, and just under the law. Man must eat in order to pray. To set off the two spheres, temporal and spiritual, in an artificial manner is wrong in theory and impossible of realization. The state will either be friendly to religion or hostile—there is no middle ground. The Catholic also rejects the idea that religion is the expression of a national spirit and that it is English, French, German, or Spanish. As has been said, the Church's intent is not primarily in the *polis* but in the *cosmopolis*. The Catholic does not accept the idea of the Church as just another social organization like a club or fraternal order, a chamber of commerce, or a labor union. The Church conceives of herself as a perfect society, just as the state is, but having an end more important for man than any purely human organization. The Catholic believes that his Church is *one* and *holy*, that it is the one means chosen by Christ for the salvation of men. While not denying that other religious groups have much of the truth, and not denying to their sincere members the salvation that Christ desires for all men, the Catholic Church teaches that it has the complete deposit of truth necessary for salvation and that all who are convinced of this must accept its teaching on peril of losing eternal life. Its belief is that other religious groups suffer from a defect of the whole truth in matters spiritual. The Church makes no claim to supreme and unerring knowledge in the temporal order—it does not know the last or final word in social, political, or other mundane affairs. And its knowledge of the physical universe may be as erring as anyone else's.

Without question, every believing Christian or Jew can admit the primacy of the spiritual. Here we are not referring to any church or creed. One's relationship with the Supreme Being, Creator and Lord of the Universe, in the spirit of the first commandment, supersedes all interests and all claims. To hold that the voice of the political order, whether of ruler or people, is the voice of God is idolatry theologically and totalitarianism politically. Even for the unbeliever, the concepts of the spiritual hold an unquestionable truth, for he must know from his own reason that something transcends the state. He may contend that a natural law, the rules of decency of mankind, the voice of conscience, or the whole field of the arts, the sciences, philosophy, or the domain of "spiritual rights" lie outside the state's competence. He may think of the word spiritual as touching things of the mind and convictions, or personal liberty. No one can claim total allegiance for the political order without degrading the individual personality to a condition of social servitude. The study of politics begins with a study of man and his needs and a determination of which of these needs the state can serve in the interest of the common good. Even the most enthusiastic statist must deny that the state can and should serve all the needs of man. By its very nature and in the practical order it cannot.

To the believer, however, there is an order that transcends the temporal order. As Jacques Maritain puts it: "The direct ordination of the human person to God transcends every created common good—both the common good of the political society and the intrinsic common good of the universe. Here is the rock of the dignity of the human person as well as the unshakeable requirements of the Christian message."[1] All man's activities, all of man's institutions are directed to a supra-temporal end in the long run. This does not deny to the state a place of great dignity worthy of man's service and devotion. Without it he could not live. Or, as Aristotle put it, he would have to be a beast or a god to live without it. Serving man's needs for peace, for material goods, for the pursuit of learning, for ordered social living, for the promotion of the virtues, the state ranks high in the institutions of men. It is not a necessary evil, but a positive good. And he who serves it well serves God and man. For what is ordained by nature for man is ordained by God. Yet the state— and the end it serves is subordinate to the spiritual order. The general principle laid down here does not differ from the general principle that has been generally held throughout the whole history of western thought. The principle is not abrogated by the difficulty of its application.

The superiority or supremacy of the spiritual does not mean a complete subordination of the political order to the whim of every churchman. It is a superiority of prestige and dignity and a power without arms. Undoubtedly there have been times in history when servants of the spiritual order have claimed more than has been their due. These incidents are more often magnified while the civilizing and humane influences of the spiritual power are buried in the dust of history. While no one would defend today the existence of a whole hierarchy of ecclesiastical courts independently functioning within the state, one may not deny the numberless times throughout past ages when such judicial institutions were the sole defenders of the little people against semibarbarous overlords. Too frequently we think of the horrors of the Spanish variety of the Court of the Inquisition, or churchly rule over all merriment in Puritan England, or the harsh condemnation of the erring by New England divines; these extreme situations to many may exemplify the supremacy of the spiritual. But even the Court of the Inquisition, whatever happened to it under the Spanish tyranny, was initiated as a

[1] Jacques Maritain, *Man and the State* (Chicago: The University of Chicago Press, 1950).

means for protecting people from unjust accusation of heresy on the part of the irresponsible leaders of the mob.

The danger today does not lurk in the claims of ecclesiastical power, but in the claims of the temporal power. Neither the Catholic Church nor any other church can stand up against the power of the state. May it not even be said that in actual practice we have today a supremacy of the temporal power? The forces of religion are indeed strong when mobilized in most northern countries of the west, but people everywhere have developed a cautious attitude in mixing the political and the religious. How the principle of the supremacy of the spiritual shall be effectuated in our times remains a problem for every religious group. Later on we shall see how the Catholics regard the application of this principle.

The second principle from the Catholic point of view is freedom for the Church in the sphere of its work—freedom to administer the sacraments, freedom to preach and teach, freedom to engage in missionary enterprise, freedom to worship, freedom in its own internal government. Considering its position as the Church founded by Christ, it is ordered to seek this freedom. It must oppose by the spiritual means at hand every obstacle placed in the way of this freedom. In recent times, this freedom has been curtailed to a considerable degree in Scandinavian countries, in lands under the Orthodox Church and in Moslem countries. The curtailment has, however, been most extreme under the totalitarian regimes. Even under restrictive regimes, the Church seeks to work and adapt itself, knowing that it may not, even under unpopular types of government, surrender its mission for the care of souls. This last point has often been misunderstood in recent years when the Church has worked in lands under political tyrannies. It has been charged that this adaptability has meant approval of totalitarian systems, but in such cases the Church, without setting its seal of approval on the regime, has kept its sights on the people whose spiritual needs it must care for even under difficulties. It never feels that it can ask the supreme sacrifice of freedom and life from the great masses of the people by throwing them headlong into warfare with a political system. Obviously, this does not mean that it will sacrifice the fundamental principles of Christianity in exchange for any favors from the powers that be. One of the secrets of the success of the Church throughout the ages has been its adaptability to conditions most unfavorable to its work; yet it has kept the nature of its primary mission clearly in view. With complete freedom or with little freedom, it will work, but its *right* to complete freedom, it will not deny.

Believing Christians and Jews seek a like freedom; the Jews, however, would say that they have no missionary doctrine to follow. Unbelievers will often see the basic justification for this freedom if they recognize the right of the person to follow his convictions, to organize for the purpose, and peacefully to try to convince others of their points of view. They will be favorable to the concept that diversity in opinion in the body politic leads to a richer social life, provided, of course, the opinion does not lead to the undermining of the social and political order.

The third principle may be termed co-operation. In the modern era, this principle is the most generally misunderstood. In the strict sense, co-operation and separation are not compatible terms. A constitutional principle of the separation of powers exists in the American system of government in which executive, legislative, and judicial functions are defined as distinct and as holding specific areas of power, but no one thinks of the President as sitting at one end of Pennsylvania Avenue aloof and cut off from Congress at the other end. We normally think of the term separation as meaning a severance of all the relations, official or otherwise. Unfortunately, that is the unrealistic sense in which some people interpret the phrase "separation of church and state." Dr. Reinhold Niebuhr has rightly said: "I do not think the Founding Fathers stood for an absolute wall of separation of Church and State. . . . I think we have to reject the idea that there can be an absolute wall of separation between Church and State. We cannot accept this because both Church and State today articulate the community in its various functions. Ways must be found in which Church and State do co-operate, provided there be no specific advantage to one religion over another."[2]

At a thousand points the members of churches and sometimes

[2] Reprinted in *Catholic Mind*, Feb., 1952.

the churches themselves meet the government, and for the most part in co-operation. If the term *separation* means that the Church should not get itself involved in the myriad forms of politics—directing, advising, using influence through the spoils system, or enmeshing itself in the temporal affairs which properly belong to the state, then every reasonable person can agree that separation is good. There can and should be an area, considering religion in general, not the Catholic Church alone, midway between the solitary aloofness implied in separation and total involvement, in which churches can and should carry out their mission. But to the Catholic, the principle of co-operation logically follows from the other principles of the primacy of the spiritual and the necessary freedom of the Church.

It should be remembered that the end of the state is the common good. The ends pursued by man are, however, not so separated that one does not impinge upon or include the other. We may, for instance, talk about two separate disciplines such as theology and philosophy, but at some points the borders of each touch; or we may consider physics and chemistry, and yet the first principles of the latter are found in the former. As in the fields of knowledge, so in the realm of man's end or purpose in life—an order of values exists for him and one value may overlap the other or one value may be basic for the other. Or in another context—I cannot pray and serve God unless I have food, clothing, and shelter. And it has often been pointed out that most often Christ healed physical infirmities first and then preached the good message of salvation.' So the common good of the state is not unrelated to the transcendent common good of man. In a well-ordered state which respects the freedom and dignity of man, the citizen rightly pursuing his supra-temporal end should be an exemplary citizen. I do not mean to say that the religious person is always a good citizen, but normally the good man in the good state is a good citizen. A religious people will respect the laws and support a just government. But if this is so, it will be done, as St. Augustine long ago pointed out, because the obedience to a temporal order serves a supra-temporal end.

In the modern period, the state touches the people and institutions at so many points that it becomes ever more difficult to determine where the line of division between the temporal and spiritual power should be drawn. At no time is politics unrelated to morals. The city authority that does nothing to eliminate crime-breeding slums or takes lightly the existence of brothels, or the government that fosters an unjust economic system or conceives of atomic developments mainly for the purpose of destruction or promotes prosperity for a few while a large portion of the people starve places itself squarely athwart the fundamental teaching of Judaeo-Christian thought. Many governmental problems are complex indeed and the aim of the specialist may run counter to the aims of the moralist. Yet there are people who deny to churchmen even freedom of religious protest, so rigorously do they apply the separation doctrine. This is the new intolerance of our day. Not infrequently, however, people who criticize such "interference" in secular affairs are more stirred by a position in opposition to their own than in any violation of the accepted relations between religious and political leaders.

For a Catholic what does this principle of co-operation between church and state mean? Obviously, it may take various forms, but the principle remains. Historical situations do not make or unmake the principle. While the Catholic may not accept the historicism that teaches that time and condition create morals, he knows that the peace and good order of the political community is a pearl of great price and he would be loath indeed to impose what he believes to be a perfect order upon a reluctant community. It has frequently been pointed out that the great error of the leaders of the French Revolution was the effort to impose utopian schemes of government upon a people neither desiring nor prepared for them. Leaders so motivated will take to coercive measures readily to compel the people to conform.

Now the Catholic, realizing the great values of his faith, would like to see everyone within this One Fold with One Shepherd. He does not fear that this unity would create uniformity. He feels that Christ himself set down certain essential beliefs, and that these are beneficial for all men both here and hereafter. And he believes that his Church has all the essential means for directing men in the way of everlasting truth. But he has neither the desire nor the right to impose those beliefs on anyone. He is taught that even an erroneous conscience must be respected. St. Thomas taught this in an age when most of his contemporaries were reluctant to put the principle into practice. If the conscience of man is inviolate, there remains in addition the law of charity, which knows no bounds—it must be extended to all men.

Whatever co-operation, therefore, exists between church and state, these principles must be observed. We no longer live in an age of powerful monarchs who hold the destinies of nations in their hands. Political wisdom now recognizes the worth of the individual, the basic equality of men, their political responsibility, and their title to participation in affairs of the state. The answerability of governments to popular control is a fundamental constitutional principle in most of the leading nations of the world. The lofty principles of democracy, while nowhere fully realized, form the goals toward which the people strive. In this day any co-operation must have a popular support. With the three principles already discussed clearly in view, the possible forms of co-operation must fully respect social conditions. In a Catholic political order, these forms will vary, whether incorporated in a concordat or tacitly understood.

In a society *overwhelmingly* Catholic, a public recognition of the Roman Catholic faith as the religion of the state and the people would ordinarily be expected. Public ceremonies would be accompanied with Catholic forms of worship. What would be expected beyond this would be a matter to be determined in each state according to custom and tradition. Yet it should be kept in mind that Catholics have grown in knowledge and wisdom in matters political just as Protestants have. Certain institutional arrangements of another age do not and never can fit our own or any time in the foreseeable future. This is not the thirteenth century, and we have to come to a realization that every man must be respected in that sphere, the spiritual, in a way that befits his dignity as a citizen and as child of the One God and Father of all. People today justly recall days of religious persecution and violence which constitute a scandalous page in the history of religion. Restrictions on the activities of men in the sphere that is the most sacred to him, whether these restrictions are peaceful or strongly coercive, do not in the long run serve the cause of peace and justice. Thus even in a state with a large Catholic majority, it would surely not be part of wisdom to restrict non-Catholics to second-class citizenship, which would restrict their preaching and teaching or would deny their equal status before the law.

With regards to coercion in matter of faith, Pope Pius XII said:

Though we desire this unceasing prayer to rise to God from the whole Mystical Body in common, that all the straying sheep may enter the one fold of Jesus Christ, yet We recognize that this must be done of their own free will; for no one believes unless he wills to believe. Hence they are most certainly not genuine Christians who against their belief are forced to go into a church, to approach the altar and to receive the Sacraments; for the 'faith without which it is impossible to please God' is an entirely free 'submission of intellect and will.' Therefore whenever it so happens, despite the constant teaching of this Apostolic See, that anyone is compelled to embrace the Catholic faith against his will, Our sense of duty demands that We condemn the act. (*Mystici Corporis,* para. 104)

The Catholic position was well put years ago by Cardinal Manning of England when he wrote to Prime Minister Gladstone: "If Catholics were in power tomorrow in England not a penal law would be proposed, not a shadow of constraint put upon the faith of any man. We would that all men fully believed in the truth; but a forced faith is a hypocrisy hateful to God and man. . . . If the Catholics were tomorrow the 'Imperial race' in these kingdoms they would not use political power or molest the divided and hereditary religious state of the people. We should not shut one of their Churches, or Colleges, or Schools. They would have the same liberties we enjoy as a minority."[3] Only a few years ago Archbishop McNicholas of Cincinnati made a similar statement for the Catholics of the United States when he said:

"No group in America is seeking union of church and state; and least of all are Catholics. We deny absolutely and without any qualification that the Catholic Bishops of the United States are seeking a union of church and state by any endeavors whatsoever, either proximate or remote. If tomorrow Catholics constituted a

[3] Henry E. Manning *The Vatican Decrees and Their Bearing on Civil Allegiance* (London, 1875), pp. 93-96.

majority of our country, they would not seek a union of church and state. They would then as now, uphold the Constitution and all its Amendments, recognizing the moral obligation imposed on all Catholics to observe and defend the Constitution and its Amendments."

More recently, Archbishop Egidio Vagnozzi, Apostolic Delegate to the United States, in an address delivered at Loyola University, Chicago, on March 18, 1960, declared:

"In practice, the Church will not interfere, and has not interfered, in local situations where the separation between Church and State may be considered the greater and more general good.

"In considering freedom as applied to religious belief and worship, it is well to remind ourselves that the very concept of complete separation between Church and State is a relatively modern idea. Even some of the largest Protestant denominations were born out of a stricter and more nationalistic interpretation of a close relationship between religion and the civil power.

"In the practical field of relations with civil powers, the Catholic Church shows, with reciprocal international agreements called Concordats, a considerable variety of provisions in particular questions, depending on local traditions, customs and practices. In fact, it is extremely difficult to define the neat line of demarcation between the domain of the Church and that of the State. Actually, even in some traditionally and predominantly Catholic countries, no preferential juridical recognition is granted to the Catholic Church.

"As far as the United States is concerned, I feel that it is a true interpretation of the feelings of the Hiearchy and of American Catholics in general to say that they are well satisfied with their Constitution and pleased with the fundamental freedom enjoyed by their Church; in fact, they believe that this freedom is to a large extent responsible for the expansion and consolidation of the Church in this great country.

"Whether they remain a minority or become a majority, I am sure that American Catholics will not jeopardize their cherished religious freedom in exchange for a privileged position."

To a Catholic, so-called interconfessional peace is essential to a realization of the common good. The principle of the common good is of the utmost importance to Catholics. For the sake of that principle, respect would have to be shown for the diversity of religious practices. It must be noted that this respect stems from a specific principle and not from opportunism. In the very center of Roman Catholicism, Rome itself, Father de la Brière wrote these words concerning a Catholic political regime: "To attempt to impose by law, in any country, one religious cult alone or to exclude any (always reserving the rights due public order and morality) would constitute an unreasonable, chimeric, and evil venture . . . because the operation would be disastrous, violent, fatal to the social good and to civil concord; all the more so because it would touch upon the most profound, the most delicate sensibilities. Let us acknowledge that, apart from any alleged right of error, and apart also from the danger of failure in such an attempt, *there exists a serious moral reason, which forces the conclusion that compulsion in this area must be rejected today in the name of the common good.* This concept of the common good is an eminently admissible and helpful concept. It greatly illuminates the question of civil toleration, i.e., the question of the legal freedom of dissident cults, even in countries where Catholics might perhaps have sufficient power to escape that freedom.

"In the Medieval world and in Europe of old, consideration of the common good might often have worked *against* the legal freedom of dissident cults. But in the world today, considerations of the temporal common good militate *for* that freedom . . . the psychological and moral condition of society demands in the name of public tranquility and the public interest, that the legal freedom of all cults be recognized everywhere as a universal rule of civilization—public order and public morality always being safeguarded. *For all nations this is a matter of universal obligation and mutual good faith.*"[4]

Official statements of the Catholic Church are never flamboyant. They are marked by a certain caution that will never satisfy the young man in a hurry. The Church moves slowly, with due regard for the established habits of men. It takes human nature as it finds it and does its best to perfect it. It does the same with man's institutions. While it is not primarily an authority in politics, it holds as true what Aristotle taught centuries ago that politics is a science of the contingent in which the chief

[4] *Miscellanea Vermeersch* (Rome: 1935), Vol. II, pp. 174-85.

virtue is prudence. With the restraint typical of the Church, Pius XII said in a discourse to the Italian Jurists (December 6, 1953): "The duty of repressing moral and religious error cannot therefore be an ultimate norm of action. It must be subordinate to higher and more general norms, which, in some circumstances permit, and even seem to indicate as the better policy, toleration of error in order to promote a greater good."

Some critics of the Church's position want not only a detailed relationship of church and state, but a declaration of absolute freedom in matters of religion. It should be obvious that the Church will not and cannot formulate a Platonic ideal, down to the last details, of what a perfect church and state relationship should be. It is a universal institution and it respects the special characteristics of peoples and nations. It should be remembered that in so far as the World Council of Churches represents the thinking of world Protestantism, it has not given its special blessing to church-state relationships as established by law in the United States or to any mode of relationship. The Catholic Church cannot recognize "absolute freedom" in religious belief and practice any more than any other responsible institution can. Freedom is indeed precious, but it is a means to an end, and its exercise is judged by the nature of the end. No matter how important polygamy was as a tenet of the Mormons, neither the United States government nor American society was willing to sanction its exercise. The law of our land recognizes that man is free, but at the same time, he is responsible for the manner in which he exercises his freedom. Freedom for a purpose makes sense, but freedom for freedom's sake is nonsense.

It is difficult to imagine Catholics, in countries where it has not been traditionally the practice to support the Church or the clergy, giving support to such a policy in the name of co-operation. And the Church respects custom and tradition. In one country where this had been the tradition (Portugal) the Church voluntarily renounced the practice but a few years ago. Catholic clergymen may differ on this matter, according to the custom of the land in which they live, but large numbers of them realize the peril of being tied to the political whims of governments. No form of control is stronger than the financial, and when the whole operation of religious institutions depends upon the state treasury, their independence is jeopardized and may even be completely destroyed. It is significant that the constitution of the Republic of Ireland, after recognizing the primacy of the Catholic religion, contains the following provision: "The state guarantees not to endow any religion." This is followed by the statement "The State shall not impose any disabilities or make any discrimination on the grounds of religious profession, belief or status." (Art. 44, section 2).

With a Catholic-majority population it is conceivable that some Catholic beliefs would be incorporated in the law. Here, of course, one has to assume that all Catholics in a democratic state would think alike on the prudence of placing on the statute books an article of their creed—an assumption that might be wide of the mark. In a thoroughgoing Methodist community we might reasonably expect that liquor, gambling, and Sunday amusements of a commercial nature would be banned. In a Jewish community, it is likely that Saturday would be the day of rest by law. In a Christian Science community, one can only speculate what might be the restriction on medical practice. In all these matters, we can only posit as a guarantee against the extreme the reasonableness of men. Catholics have as their guide the wisdom of St. Thomas on Law, where he says: "Hence it is necessary that even laws may be imposed on men according to their condition: for as Isidore puts it (Etym.Bk.V,c.21) law must be possible, both with regard to nature and to the fatherland's custom. . . . Now human law is laid down for the multitude, the major part of which is composed of men not perfected by virtue. Consequently, all and every vice, from which virtuous men abstain, is not prohibited by human law, but only the gravest vicious actions . . . which are harmful to others. . . . [human law] does not immediately impose on the multitude of the imperfect those things which are required from already virtuous men, so that they would be obliged by the law to abstain from every kind of evil. Otherwise imperfect people, being unable to bear such obligations, would plunge into worse evils. . . .' Now Augustine says, "the law which is framed for the government of states allows and leaves unpunished many things that are punished by divine providence . . . wherefore, too, human law does not prohibit everything that is forbidden by the natural law.' "[5]

The application of principles to concrete situations is always a matter of practical wisdom or procedures. So it can be said:

> The natural law reflects an objective order of essences to be realized and maintained. Its content is grasped by speculative intellect. Natural-law precepts, unlike human laws, are not the product of human practical reason but are the first principles which direct it. They are thus the measures of human laws which are means for rationalizing society and bringing it to accord with the objective moral order. . . . But that does not mean that whatever it explicitly or implicitly dictates can fitly or justly be commanded by positive law as well. Natural law for example, forbids lying; the positive law does not and could not. . . . Human law, being the work of practical reason, must resign itself to limitations. . . . Man's specific perfections and dignity are found in his liberty. This is of course to be understood not of the mere physical power to choose between right and wrong, which is only the foundation and condition of *true* liberty. We mean rather the power and vision to ratify by his own will the ends of divine Wisdom and to contribute consciously to his own perfection. . . . In this perspective it can be seen that law like society itself must be in the final sense of freedom. And since every human law implies restraint and may often curtail liberties otherwise justly exercised, it can be justified only because it promotes another and more urgent liberty.[6]

In other words, the very nature of positive law prevents either the Catholic, the Protestant, or the Jew from setting up a utopia according to his ideals. The ultimate beliefs of all the religious groups aim at the moral integrity of the individual, but this is of no concern to the positive law unless justice is involved. And justice is *par excellence* a social virtue. If the law prevents drunkenness or theft, it is not to make a person moral; it is to prevent dangers to society. The common good is the aim of law.

This is not to deny that an individual's morality does not affect the common good. A man's laziness may affect the common good, it is true, or his bad habit of lying, but the law can only reach

[5] *Summa Theologica*, 1-11, 96.
[6] Rev. Vincent J. Dolan, S.J., "Thèse Philosophique de Laval, No. 1007," *Natural Law and Modern Jurisprudence* (Quebec: Laval University, 1958), pp. 208-9.

external acts as they very directly affect society. The common good involves spiritual values. The private morality of citizens does affect the common good. So it may be that a religious group might wish with all its heart that all men follow its precepts and might be tempted as people were in other ages to incorporate its beliefs in positive law, yet it is seeking to do the impossible and the unjust. Not all Catholics, all Protestants, and all Jews throughout the world fully realize this. For the Catholics, however, it should be kept in mind that it is quite consonant with their own basic teachings. To many non-Catholics, the laws governing morals in many Catholic countries appear lax—and incidently they appear lax to many Catholics of Irish descent—but they follow faithfully the rule that laws must fit the conditions that can best be dealt with by positive law.

Despite the position of law as striking the lowest common denominator of what a people will accept, it is educative, and it does become the legislator's task to raise the standards of a community, but cautiously. "Laws must be such as the greater majority of men find easy to obey."[7] A society must make progress and the low standards of a few should not hold it back.

The late Justice Cardoza said:

"One mind in the right, whether in statesmanship, science, morals, or what not, may raise all other minds to its own point of view. We do not strike an average between the thoughts of ability and folly. If it is not the commonplace, still less is it the hasty prepossession, the whim or humor of the hour. Rather are we to identify it with that strong and preponderant opinion which has capacity at times to turn desire into law."[8]

It should be remembered, however, considering the Catholic Church's respect for long-established custom in any place, that if the United States ever, by a large majority of the people, became Catholic, "It would mean, of course, an arrangement that took account of the spirit of American institutions as formed by history, tradition, and custom. American Protestantism, as a historical phenomenon, would always and inevitably be part of the background of American Catholicism. Beyond that there is

[7] Dolan, *op. cit.*
[8] Quoted in Dolan, *op. cit.*, pp. 240-41.

no point in speculating on what posterity is to do in circumstances we can only abstractly contemplate."[9]

It is not possible to predict what any electorate will do with
their suffrage in any future condition. All men, Protestant, Catholic, Jew, and unbeliever, may at times do foolish and unwise
things with their votes. As Montesquieu says: "Sometimes with
a hundred thousand arms they [the people] overturn all before
them; and sometimes with a hundred thousand feet they creep
like insects."[10] Non-Catholics might ask what Catholics would do
in a Catholic society on birth control; it is impossible to say.
They are not responsible for the birth-control legislation in the
two states of the United States where contraceptive information
is prohibited (Massachusetts and Connecticut). All Catholics
agree that mechanical means to prevent conception are against
the natural law, but not all agree as to the wisdom of legislative prohibition—this despite the opposition of Catholics in
Massachusetts and Connecticut to the repeal of such laws. In no
state where such laws are lacking have Catholics made any move
to incorporate them into statutes—even where Catholics are a
large part of the electorate. The feelings of many Catholics on
this subject are indicated by the sentence already quoted from
St. Thomas: "Human law does not prohibit everything that is
forbidden by the natural law." It is hardly within the realm of
the conceivable that a Catholic state would establish birth-control clinics. On divorce it is possible that a Catholic state would
not recognize such a practice at all or more likely would judge
each case according to the religious convictions of the parties
involved. In the American federal system, however, these are
matters of state determination, not of federal control.

It is likely that in a Catholic state co-operation would involve
some kind of aid to Catholic education. But if one may judge
from present practice in Catholic states, this aid would be available to non-Catholic groups as well. Here Catholics would have
to be mindful of what has already been stated, that a close financial tie-up with the political powers has perils. While in its educational institutions, religion promotes the common good and

[9] Dolan, *op cit.*, p. 249.
[10] Baron de Montesquieu, *Spirit of the Laws,* (World's Greatest Literature,
1900) Vol. XI, pp. 9–10.

in justice may ask for state aid, yet it must ever be on its guard against those encroachments by direction or control which would greatly endanger the independence of the school and the Church alike. While the United States by law does not, most countries do give support to private and religious educational institutions. The Catholic in laying down such a requirement in a Catholic state may decide how much or how little or what forms this aid will take, but in proposing it, he does not feel that he is suggesting anything particularly new and untried. Reinhold Niebuhr has said of this practice: "There isn't a modern democratic society in Europe that does not give children (in independent schools) more tax support than we do. The whole problem would have been settled a long time ago if one had been willing to give our Catholic friends a bit. . . . I believe that Protestantism and secularism are too formally legalistic and righteous when they say that children in parish schools should not get any support at all. I do not think this is realistic. . . ."[11]

It is likely, too, in a Catholic country, that the laws would punish insult or scorn to religion, as they do in such a free country as Switzerland, the guilt in such cases being based upon the kind of language used and the intention of the user to give offense. Such laws without question would apply to all religious groups. I am not unaware that the existence of such laws in certain Catholic countries has operated against a few Protestant missionary groups which use an especially offensive propaganda against Catholic beliefs. Not only law, but simple good manners should dictate the behavior of religious groups in any country. The modern technique of blaring loudspeakers throwing insults at fundamental Catholic beliefs is not kindly received in an overwhelmingly Catholic society, nor would this clumsy form of propaganda against Protestant beliefs be calmly accepted in a society fundamentally Protestant. This would not, however, condone the practice of individual or mob violence against such boorish behavior.

* In summing up the consideration of the Catholic position on church and state, it should be made clear that Catholics regard the three principles of primacy of the spiritual, the freedom of

[11] *Columbia* (June, 1951).

the Church, and the necessity of co-operation between church and state as the essential principles to be maintained. In the words of Maritain: "As concerns my attempt to outline a future type of Christian political society, whatever one may think of its particular features, what matters essentially to me is the fact that the supreme general principles are immutable; and that the ways of applying, of realizing them are analogical, and change according to the variety of historical climates. So the principles which were applied in a given way by the sacral civilization of the Middle Ages always hold true, but they are to be applied in another way in modern secular civilization."[12]

In accordance with the requirements of the present day, Cardinal Carejeria, Patriarch of Lisbon, commenting on the new concordat between the Holy See and Portugal, stated the thinking of increasing numbers of Catholics when he said: "The Portuguese State recognizes the Church as she is, and ensures her freedom; but she does not support or protect her as a state established religion. . . . What the Church loses in official protection, she gains in virginal freedom of action. Free from any liability toward political power, her voice gains greater authority upon consciences. She leaves Caesar a complete clear field in order for herself better to attend to the things that are of God. She is the pure crystal from which the treasure of the Christian revelation is streaming forth."[13]

In a pluralistic society, particularly a democratic society, Catholics recognize the political equality established for all religions. Whether Justice Douglas's words were obiter dicta or otherwise, they stated an indubitable fact that we are a religious people. Catholics hold, therefore, that in a society of believers possessing a Judaeo-Christian heritage, public acknowledgment of the existence of the Creator and our dependence upon Him is required. In such a society, within the bounds of the maintenance of the public order, freedom of religious practice in the forms customary in our land is definitely required. In general, Catholics hold, since the state is not able to determine religious truth, a benevolent neutrality on the part of public authority toward religion is a requirement in justice.

[12] J. Maritain, *op. cit.*, pp. 179-80.
[13] J. Maritain, *op. cit.*, quoted.

In the establishment of policy in a pluralistic society Catholics will have the same voice as others in proclaiming a point of view, in seeking its adoption by peaceful means, and in voting their convictions. The Church will have the same right (as other institutions) to make effective its point of view on public affairs. It is here understood that the means used will be in accordance with the accepted methods of the democratic order and in accordance with the dignity that befits the Church's nature.

What of certain beliefs that Catholics hold which they deem necessary for the common good, such as measures against euthanasia, easy divorce, or abortion? Because these policies may be democratically approved, does not mean that they are morally right. The voice of the people is not the voice of God, and the state is not the creator of moral principles. The Church looks upon it as a duty to oppose measures of this kind which it believes harmful to all individuals and disastrous to the common good. Under democratic principles, its clergy as citizens and its members may not be denied the right of opposition and all the means of opposition that the democratic process affords. This is not to say that the action of Catholic clergy, or societies, or parishes, or members has always been dictated by prudence. And the unfortunate reputation which Catholics have in some circles is due to too many loud and noisy actions on the side of prohibitions. When these actions are sustained by boycotts, picketing, or too great a zeal for censorship, our fellow citizens are apt to conclude that with us the appeal to action takes precedence over the appeal to reason. Such action, too, leads men to believe that the Church knows nothing but restrictions and prohibitions. The bishops of the Church will always be slow to take an official position on public questions, but this is not always true of all clergy or all prominent laymen. At the slightest provocation the latter declare an *official* position of the Church which many non-Catholics accept as genuine. The practice of "throwing one's weight around," indulged in from time to time by some groups in the Church, does irreparable harm to the cause of peace, good will, and understanding.

One diocese, one parish, or one organization of laymen, however prominent, does not necessarily speak for the Catholic Church.

In the world, few are the political societies that are not pluralistic. Even in some states which are usually called Catholic, attachment to the Catholic faith is very tenuous or hardly exists among large numbers of the people. Yet in modern society the Church has gained in the number of her adherents intelligently attached to the faith. The freedom accorded to the Church in pluralistic societies has increased rather than decreased the number of her loyal followers. The sacral age has gone, but a new age of greater independence of the Church is in progress. The Church will accommodate itself to this age in a manner born of the wisdom of the centuries and of her knowledge of men. In this accommodation no man should fear for his rights as a responsible person in the sight of God.

CHAPTER IV

The Confused State of the Law

While the eighteenth and nineteenth century saw the incorporation of provisions relating to church and state in constitutional and statutory law, the twentieth century thus far has been characterized by fitting the law to new problems. It has been an era of interpretation. Considering the rapidly expanding field of government, both state and federal, this trend was inevitable. The question of aid to parochial schools stands out as the most conspicuous of the problems, but questions relating to the taxation of church property, Sunday closing laws, censorship of the movies and literature, United States representation at the Vatican, and legislation on birth control also figure.

The difficulties of fitting legal theory to existing practice and traditions are nowhere better illustrated than in the United States. We have a law that says one thing on the relation of church to state, a slogan that says another thing, and commonly accepted practices that contradict both. Difficulty especially arises from attempts to draw a strict line of division between government and religion in a society that is fundamentally religious either by inheritance or by practice. I have said elsewhere that there can be no neat division into the temporal and supra-temporal—especially in a believing society. When one looks carefully at the motive behind present-day separation of the two, one may safely say that freedom of religion is the aim, not restriction of religion. Our difficulties would appear to stem from our great concern with the latter almost to the exclusion of the former.

Our history is replete with official references to God, with respectful governmental treatment of religion, and to governmental use of religious groups for the promotion of the general welfare. Constitutional government in America begins "In the name of God" in the Mayflower compact; with a firm reliance on the protection of "Divine Providence" the colonists declared their independence from Great Britain; the framers of the preambles of the new state constitutions thank Almighty God for the blessings of freedom He has bestowed; the First Congress provides means for the conversion of the Indians to Christianity. President Jefferson, author of the wall of separation, uses government funds to support a Catholic priest and to build a chapel for the welfare of the Indians; all sessions of Congress open with a supplication to the Creator; the United States Supreme Court begins its sessions with "God save the United States and this honorable court"; the President calls upon Americans once a year to repair to their houses of worship to thank God for his blessings; the clergy are exempted from military service; and churches are exempt from taxes.

All these things may prove nothing from the legal point of view but they do demonstrate that Americans have a deep respect for religion, and since this is the case, the building of a wall of separation would not seem to mean the dropping of an iron curtain between the government and religion. While the constitution allows no religious test for office, it is difficult to imagine the electorate of the nation or any state electing to office a declared agnostic or atheist. We expect our presidents to go to church even when they have not been regular churchgoers before taking office. If history demonstrates anything, it demonstrates that our main interest has been in religious liberty and not in separating the government from the influence of religion or even from the fostering of it.

From the numerous cases involving Jehovah's Witnesses we may note how alert the Supreme Court has been to protect religious groups from governmental interference. We have, however, entered in recent years into a new phase of judicial interpretation in which the emphasis has been on the restrictive phrases of the First and Fourteenth Amendments. The court decisions—state and federal—conflicting as they are, have not enlightened even the keenest of legal minds.

Matters have not been improved by an emotion-charged atmosphere among the people themselves, whose thinking has frequently been confused by the use of the slogan: Separation of church and state. Neither the state nor federal constitutions use the phrase. Often in the democratic process we find the emotive word or slogan made use of to cover up any deep analysis of a question. Consider a list of some of them: fascism, communism, free enterprise, no entangling alliances, socialized medicine, radical, reactionary. One could multiply these several times over. Each one of these creates a stereotype in the mind which only partly reflects reality. When the words separation of church and state are combined with Roman Church or Catholic Church, lurid imagination takes over and thinking comes to an end for some of our fellow citizens.

The danger of the constant use of a slogan comes from its producing effects not anticipated. As a people we went through the period of laissez-faire individualism emphasizing free enterprise while great concentrations of capital were building up, trusts and combines that stifled the very thing we were praising. The Supreme Court was most solicitous in protecting the fictitious person, the corporation, while forgetting the person of flesh and blood. We reached the point of absurdity in this period with the Supreme Court decision in the Lochner Case (1905) when Justice Peckham, anxious about the system of "free" contract between an employer and an employee, could not see any harm in a baker working more than ten hours a day because no harm was done to the bread! I could readily conceive of a time when separation of church and state would become such a thoughtless slogan that only rights of the state would be left and the church would effectively be denied the means of operating. Aligned with some religious people in the current separation battles are secularists who are not simply indifferent to religion but hold convictions, tantamount to a religious faith, which are hostile to religion. The latter are dangerous allies; they are more clear in their minds as to what they want than their religious-minded affiliates.

The legal situation regarding church and state in this country has been ably surveyed by Protestant, Catholic, and Jewish scholars. The author, as a political scientist and Catholic, begs the reader's patience while he takes a look at the problem.

The constitution as originally drawn contains one sentence on the subject of religion which provides that "no religious test shall ever be required as a qualification to any office or public trust under the United States" (Article VI). At the demand of the states after the adoption of the constitution ten amendments (the Bill of Rights) were passed by the First Congress and approved by the necessary number of states. The first of them provides that "Congress shall make no law respecting an establishment of religion or prohibiting the free exercise thereof." This clause was produced after a number of attempts at arriving at a satisfactory guarantee were made. James Madison, who took a leading part in framing the Bill of Rights of the Constitution, proposed that the clause on religion should read as follows:

> The civil rights of none should be abridged on account of religious belief or worship, nor shall any national religion be established, nor shall the full and equal rights of conscience be in any manner, or on any pretext, infringed.

The forces behind the adoption of the amendment included the representatives from states with established churches (There were five such states: Massachusetts, Connecticut, South Carolina, New Hampshire, and Maryland) who wanted to protect the state arrangments from interference by Congress; the representation of smaller religious groups who feared the establishment of one of the larger Protestant groups as the official religion; Baptist groups who had firm convictions which were opposed to any kind of church establishment, and an elite group, small but powerful, who had absorbed the dogmas of the Enlightenment. Madison explained what he sought by the amendment:

> He apprehended the meaning of the words to be, that Congress should not establish a religion . . . nor compel men to worship God in any manner contrary to their conscience. . . . If the word *national* was inserted before religion, it would satisfy the minds of honorable gentlemen. . . . He thought if the word national was introduced, it would point the amendment directly to the object it was intended to prevent.[1]

The main purpose behind the amendment was to secure religious liberty and to prevent any action by the congress which would impair this liberty. The amendment did not apply to

---

[1] *Annals of Congress*, I, CC 758-59.

action by the states. It should be remembered, however, that as John Bennett says: "But it cannot be too strongly emphasized that the American system of Church-State separation was not the result of hostility to Christianity or of the desire to put the Churches at a disadvantage. It was the result of the competition of many Churches and of the sincere belief of many churchmen that Churches were better off when they were on their own."[2]

The first ten amendments to the Constitution of the United States restrict the action of Congress. They do not restrict the state governments. The first amendment begins with the words: "Congress shall make no law." For many years it was assumed that the Bill of Rights of the state constitutions protected individuals sufficiently from state actions.

The fourteenth amendment to the Constitution, adopted in 1868 and having for one of its main purposes the protection of the newly freed Negroes of the South, imposed extensive restrictions on the states. The portion of special interest on the religious question reads: "No state shall make or enforce any law which shall abridge the privileges or immunities of citizens of the United States; nor shall any state deprive any person of life, liberty, or property, without due process of law; nor deny to any person within its jurisdiction the equal protection of the laws." The term "due process" is one of those elastic phrases of ancient lineage in English law; all that it implies has never been revealed by the Supreme Court. Volumes have been written on the subject; suffice it to say it has constituted a great protection for the person against arbitrary actions by the courts or the legislatures.

Fifty-seven years after the adoption of the Fourteenth Amendment the Supreme Court, through Mr. Justice Southerland in *Giltow v. New York* (268 US 652, 1925) gave to the amendment an interpretation which perhaps its authors did not intend. He said: "For present purposes we may and do assume that freedom of speech and of the press—which are protected by the First Amendment from abridgment by Congress—are among the fundamental personal rights and liberties protected by the due process clause of the Fourteenth Amendment from impairment by the

[2] John Bennett, *Christians and the State* (New York: Charles Scribner's Sons, 1958).

States." This opened the question of how many of the first ten amendments were included in the Fourteenth. Mr. Justice Black would say that the Fourtenth Amendment incorporates all of the Bill of Rights. Mr. Justice Cardozo, expressing the more common opinion, believed that the Fourteenth Amendment included such parts of the Bill of Rights as were necessary to a scheme of "ordered liberty." A third opinion holds that the Fourteenth Amendment includes all of the Bill of Rights but even more, not yet revealed; we do know, however, that from definite decisions of the Supreme Court the First Amendment, as it applies to a church establishment and the free exercise of religion, does come within the provisions of the Fourteenth Amendment.

Not until the present century was the Court called upon to deal extensively with cases involving religion. It has within the present generation handed down several decisions on the liberties and restrictions involved, applying them for the most part to actions by the states under the Fourteenth Amendment. It has had to decide many cases involving the religious freedom of groups and individuals on the one hand and the power over the general welfare which the states exercise. One of the first cases involved the power of a state to compel parents to send their children between the ages of eight and sixteen to the public schools. In this case the Court held unanimously that the act of the state interfered unreasonably with the liberty of parents in directing the education of their children and deprived the plaintiffs of property without due process of law.[3] There followed numerous decisions involving religious groups (most of them involved the sect of Jehovah's Witnesses) and their specific rights to propagate their religion. Thus an ordinance of New York City requiring a permit from the police commissioner before a meeting of religious groups could be held in the streets was held "clearly invalid as a prior restraint" on freedom of speech. The Court added that if the meeting had resulted in public disorder, then those responsible could be punished.[4] So also a law requiring the approval of a state official before a religious organization could solicit funds in public places was declared invalid.

[3] *Pierce* v. *Society of Sisters,* 268, US 510, 1925.
[4] *Kunz* v. *New York,* 340, US 290, 1951.

Mr. Justice Roberts in speaking for the Court declared: "Thus the Amendment [Fourteenth] embraces two concepts—freedom to believe and freedom to act. The first is absolute, but, in the nature of things, the second cannot be. . . ."[5] A New York City ordinance that required a permit for religious meetings on Sundays in the public parks when loud speakers were used was declared invalid as an unconstitutional restraint on freedom of speech and religion. The minority of the Court were willing to uphold the ordinance on the ground that loud speakers were a nuisance.[6] A city may not require a license for the distribution of religious pamphlets,[7] and while a city may forbid the distribution of handbills of advertising matter, it may not forbid the distribution of religious handbills which contain advertising.[8] Door-to-door solicitation by a religious group for the purposes of making converts may be an intolerable nuisance but it may not be prohibited by state law.[9] Acts of religious groups contrary to the peace, good order, and morals of society may definitely be prohibited.[10] Where matters of public health are concerned the states may use their powers to compel all to comply with the law despite religious scruples. And the federal government may extend as a privilege exemption from military services to citizens who oppose such service on religious grounds or to clergymen of all religious groups.

The education issue, however, has become the explosive, emotion-charged issue of the day. It is not necesary to cover the history of private and parochial education in this country. This has been adequately done. For Catholics, however, religion is an essential part of education. The Church and the home are indeed vital forces in religious education, but neither can supply that formal education which the schools give. Catholics do not deny that certain disciplines have an autonomy of their own. There is, it is true, no Catholic physics, no Catholic chemistry, no Catholic mathematics. Some Catholics deny there is a Catholic philosophy. But all disciplines are connected; the first principles

[5] *Cantwell* v. *Connecticut*, 310, US 296, 1940.
[6] *Saia* v. *New York*, 334, US 558, 1948.
[7] *Lowell* v. *City of Griffen*, 303, US 444, 1938.
[8] *Jamison* v. *Texas*, 318, US 413, 1943.
[9] *Murdock* v. *Pennsylvania*, 319, US 105, 1943.
[10] *Reynolds* v. *U.S.*, 98, US 145, 1878.

of one discipline depend upon another. And most political theorists maintain that the first principles of politics are found in ethics—strange as that may sound to some people. In all knowledge we finally get back to those basic questions for which the primary discipline of philosophy has no answers and in this realm it makes a great difference to the Catholic whether the agnostic gives the answer or the believing person. It is sad but true that in secular education even some of the best of scholars will give snap answers about a field in which they have neither training nor knowledge. The temptations to cross over into other fields always constitutes a temptation for every scholar, but for some the field of theology is the field upon which they most love to trespass. How one separates religion from the field of art, literature, history, and many of the social sciences no man has yet discovered.

The teacher hostile or neutral to religion will not readily disguise his convictions. Mr. Justice Holmes once said: "Every idea is an incitement. It offers itself for belief, and, if believed, it is acted on unless some other belief outweighs it, or some failure of energy stifles the movement at its birth. The only difference between the expression of an opinion and an incitement in the narrower sense is the speaker's enthusiasm for the result. Eloquence may set fire to reason."[11] Catholics would contend that the absence of religion from education does constitute in a way a religion in itself. They would agree with Professor Bennett's statement: "It is widely recognized that when all specific forms of religion are omitted from the world of the schools, this is itself a negative form of religious teaching; it strongly implies that religion is peripheral and dispensable as a matter of human concern." Or when he says: "The religious vacuum in public education is often filled by a religion of democracy that is thought to be more enlightened than the historic faiths. The fact that this kind of approach is not connected with any of the traditional Churches means that it can be presented in schools without being spotted as religious teaching that raises Church-State problems."[12]

[11] Dissenting opinion of Mr. Justice Holmes in *Gitlow v. New York*, 268, US 622, 1925.
[12] John C. Bennet, *op. cit.*, pp. 236-37; 238.

No greater danger to free institutions exists than the raising of a political doctrine, such as democracy, to a religion. No phase of life could escape its control. The voice of the majority would not only determine our taxes but our morals as well.[13]

The Catholic feels, therefore, that religion constitutes an essential part of education and that Catholic children should be educated in Catholic schools. At the same time he recognizes that the state, justly supervising the standards of schools, the qualification of the teachers, and to some extent the substance of the curriculum and its organization, has an interest in his schools, or, in other words, that the schools partake of a public interest. At the same time the Catholic knows that much of the subject matter taught in the Catholic schools is the same as that taught in the public schools. The school, therefore, contributes to the common good in training citizens in those subjects deemed to be essential for the proper ends of the state. In the strictest sense of the term the Catholic school cannot properly be classed as a private school. Because of the benefits derived by the state from Catholic education and because of the endeavor of the Catholic schools to fulfill the spirit and the intent of the state in following the laws laid down, the Catholic feels that some recognition in justice should be given to aid the system of education which Catholics through much self-sacrifice have built up. As Professor Rommen puts it: "It is against the principle of justice, once the parental rights in the matter of education are recognized, for the state to refuse to permit parents to use the schools according to these rights. It is against justice that parents should be taxed for the maintenance of the public schools and still be compelled to sacrifice income to make use of the rights."[14]

The states, however, have built up constitutional provisions, very often insurmountable, against any such aid. The older constitutions of the states in the east are not so restrictive. They generally confirm the principles of religious freedom. The newer constitutions forbid appropriations of tax money or public property for any church or sectarian purposes. Some prohibit the use

[13] Prof. J. L. Talmon, *The Rise of Totalitarian Democracy*, (Boston: Beacon Press, 1952).
[14] Heinrich Rommen, "Church and State," *Review of Politics*, Vol. 12, No. 3, pp. 337-38.

of public funds to support religious schools or teachers of religion. A few forbid the use of public funds "for any religious worship, exercise or institution."[15] State constitutional provisions prevent aid in almost any form for religious schools.

What has been the attitude of the United States Supreme Court? We have already said that the provisions of the First Amendment of the federal Constitution have been incorporated in the meaning of the Fourteenth Amendment. In the next significant decision, *Everson* v. *Board of Education*, (330, US 1, 1947), the Court by a four to five decision declared that the state of New Jersey could permit its local subdivisions to reimburse parents whose children go to nonprofit private and parochial schools for the bus money they spend in going to and coming from school. The case however, is not so significant for what it grants as what it declares it will not grant. Mr. Justice Black in speaking for the Court used these words: "Neither a state nor the Federal Government can pass laws which aid one religion, aid all religions, or prefer one religion over another."

The words of Justice Black furnished the prologue to the next decision in *McCollum* v. *Board of Education*, (333, US 203, 1948). According to the law of Illinois, teachers of various religious groups were permitted to come to the public school premises and allowed to give religious instruction on school time. The teachers were to be paid for their services by the several denominations taking part in the program. Children attended the religion classes upon the request of their parents. The children who did not attend were given other useful tasks such as reading—a not altogether unworthy assignment. Catholic, Jewish, and Protestant groups joined together and set up a program of religious instruction according to the terms of the Illinois law. The parents of one of the children, who decided that their child, Terry McCollum, be brought up as an atheist, claimed that young Terry was discriminated against in being made to feel as a person apart from his fellow students. Actually Terry's parents felt this separation more keenly than Terry. As Professor Sutherland says in commenting on this situation: "And indeed the degree of spiritual duress imposed on Terry McCollum when he was

[15] Paul G. Kauper, *Religion and the State University* (Ann Arbor, Mich.: University of Michigan Press, 1958), Ch. 5.

obliged to leave the classroom and read a book somewhere else while his classmates had religious instruction scarcely seems to rise to the same level as the compulsory segregation of negroes, or the extraction of evidence from a prisoner by forcible administration of an emetic."[16]

In its decision in the case the Court took particular note that the religious instruction was given on public school property. In an eight to one decision (Mr. Justice Reed dissenting) the Court declared that the Illinois law violated the separation principle since the public school system was used as a means for religious instruction.

Even Supreme Court judges should exercise great caution in entering upon the field of the trained historian. In the McCollum case the Court claimed it relied heavily on historical data. But a very good case could have been made for the State of Illinois on historical material. Certainly the people of the time of the adoption of the Constitution seemed to have no idea that religion would be separated from education, as the existing schools of the time attest. For many generations thereafter, even the public schools established throughout the land gave a good Protestant education. What Mr. Justice Black and his colleagues were doing was setting down a doctrine, dating from the mid-nineteenth century as far as education was concerned. As a doctrine of the founding fathers it could only be defended by most tortuous reasoning.

The decision blew up a veritable storm of protest. Some of the most ardent defenders of the separation idea thought this was carrying a worthy principle too far. One eminent authority on constitutional law expressed a view not uncommon among the legal fraternity when he wrote: "I personally feel that the opinions in the McCollum Case (except the dissenting opinion of Mr. Justice Reed) represented an extremist viewpoint, a doctrine of complete separation, of complete insulation of religion from the state that could stand neither an historical appraisal nor an appraisal from a common sense viewpoint of the realities."[17]

The main question which the Supreme Court had to answer in

[16] Arthur E. Sutherland, "Public Authority in the Public Schools," *Religious Education,* July–Aug., 1957.
[17] David W. Louisall, *Religious Education,* Sept.–Oct., 1955.

this case was whether the released-time program *involved an establishment of a religion of such a nature as to deprive Terry McCollum of freedom of religion.* The Fourteenth Amendment does not prevent the states from establishing religions unless they deprive people of religious liberty. Furthermore, could the Court, without stretching the meaning of the term, say that Terry was "coerced"? As Professor Edwin Corwin says: "What Terry's grievance boils down to is merely this: He felt left out in the cold because he didn't avail himself of the released-time program. But this would appear to have been his own fault. So far as anything to the contrary is shown, if Terry and his parent had made the request, the school authorities would willingly have assigned space where the two of them might have foregathered during the hour of "Released time" to confer with regard to their common-faith—or lack of it."[18]

It is even questionable whether Mrs. McCollum had enough of an interest to bring the case. She brought the suit as a taxpayer. Most lawyers know how loath the Supreme Court has been to favor taxpayer suits. While every conceivable project has been held up in the state courts on this basis, the Supreme Court has not become involved. Her paying of taxes for the maintenance of the school building seems to have given her, to say the least, a very remote interest.

The decision, based as Mr. Justice Reed wrote in his dissenting opinion upon a "figure of speech," the concept of "a wall of separation," confused rather than clarified the whole constitutional question of the relation of public-school education to religion. From any point of view it must be judged as extreme. It has piled up more unanswered questions than the Court will be able to answer with reason for a century. It would seem to indicate that among a religious people unbelief must take precedence over belief.

How has the McCollum decision been obeyed? Many communities still hold released-time classes in public-school buildings. "The most conservative estimate places noncompliances at 15 per cent of the programs, and other estimates run up to 40

[18] Edwin Corwin, "Supreme Court as School Board," *Thought,* Vol. XXIII, No. 91 (Dec.), 1948.

and 50 per cent in some states.[19] Most of the cases of non-observance appear to be in the South. Many of the programs run by the Virginia Council of Churches use public-school rooms. Many communities in Texas have religious programs in the public-school rooms. Frequently the churches pay a nominal rental for use of the school property—whether this practice evades the McCollum decision does not seem to be clear. At best it constitutes a novel evasion. The decision does not seem to have answered all questions regarding religion on public-school property—at least the people of some communities do not think so. Thus, may religious instruction be given during the lunch hour or after school hours? May high-school credit be given for Bible classes? May released-time classes be held in public community centers? May class credit be given for released time programs?[20] Many of these questions have been raised since the Zorach case which follows.

Perhaps the Supreme Court judges themselves thought they had gone too far in the McCollum case, for four years later in the case of *Zorach* v. *Clauson* (343, US 306, 1952) a milder view of religion in public-school education was evident. The Court upheld in a six to three decision a New York statute which provided that children might be released from the school premises to go to their several places of worship for religious instruction. The distinction from the McCollum case revolved around the fact that the public-school premises were not used for religious purposes. The Court was not disturbed by the fact that school time was being used. While Mr. Justice Jackson, dissenting from the majority opinion in the case, thought that under the circumstances the public school "serves as a temporary jail for a pupil who will not go to Church," Mr. Justice Douglas for the majority gave it as his opinion that: "The First Amendment, however, does not say that in every and all respects there shall be a separation of Church and State. Rather, it studiously defines the manner, the specific ways in which there shall be no concert or union or dependency one on the other. . . . Otherwise the State and Religion would be aliens to each other—hostile, suspicious,

[19] Frank J. Sorauf, "*Zorach* v. *Clauson;* The Impact of a Supreme Court Decision," *American Political Science Review,* Vol. LIII, No. 3, p. 784.
[20] Frank J. Sorauf, *op. cit.,* p. 785.

and even unfriendly. Churches could not be required to even pay property taxes. Municipalities would not be permitted to render police or fire protection to religious groups. Policemen who helped parishioners into their places of worship would violate the Constitution. Prayers in our legislative halls; appeals to the Almighty in the messages of the Chief Executive; the proclamation making Thanksgiving day a holiday; "so help me God" in our courtroom oaths—these and all other references to the Almighty that run through our laws, our public rituals, our ceremonies would be flouting the First Amendment. A fastidious atheist or agnostic could even object to the supplication with which the Court opens each session: 'God save the United States and this Honorable Court' . . . We are a religious people whose institutions presuppose a Supreme Being. . . . We find no constitutional requirement which makes it necessary for government to be hostile to religion and to throw its weight against efforts to widen the effective scope of religious influence. . . ." He also noted that we could go so far in the interpretation of the separation doctrine as to risk the danger "of preferring those who believe in no religion over those who do so believe."

Mr. Justice Douglas faces the facts of life: The American people cannot obliterate their religious convictions from their political and social thinking. Or as Professor Sutherland remarks: "The Zorach case may be taken to suggest that the Supreme Court will not undertake to protect the people of a state against every chemical trace of spiritual embarrassment from public authority."[21]

Following the Zorach decision, released-time programs were voted down in New Hampshire, Michigan, and Arizona. Thirteen states have laws permitting absence for religious instruction (California, Indiana, Iowa, Kentucky, Maine, Massachusetts, Minnesota, New York, North Dakota, Oregon, Pennsylvania, South Dakota, and West Virginia). In many states, however, it is assumed that in the absence of any legal prohibition of released time, localities may go ahead with the program. In fact, one authority wrote following the decision: "It is now the 'unalienable right' of every parent of a public-school child, if he so requests it, to have his child excused for 'religious observance and educa-

[21] *Religious Education*, July–Aug., 1957, p. 43.

tion.' In no state or local community can this right be denied."[22]

The courts have used the Zorach case to cover a multitude of various situations. In Massachusetts Bible-reading in the public schools was upheld. In Kentucky the teaching of religious orders in the public schools was upheld. In Tennessee the court held that reciting the Lord's Prayer, reading a verse from the Bible, or singing an 'inspiring song' in the public schools did not violate the doctrine of separation of church and state. In California the court ruled that tax exemption for religious property did not violate the federal Constitution.[23] The Zorach case traveled a long way through judicial decision. Strict constructionists of the separation of church and state doctrine would, I presume, vigorously assert it left a muddy trail.

It would seem, however that the public schools are free to be neutral, but that they do not have to be strangers to religion. How these two positions are to be maintained is not as yet clear. Let us say that a well-meaning teacher in the eighth grade tells her class that in this country one is free to follow any religion one chooses. Outside of the religious angle the statement falls short of the truth in that all religious practice falls within the limits of law and order. As the statement stands it might well mean that in religious matters one can follow any whim of the moment. Now as far as the state is concerned this is true, but does it square with the religious belief of many Christians and Jews who base religious belief on reasoned conviction? To the immature it might mean that one could choose a different religion for each day in the year—for surely there are enough religious groups in this country to fit such a pattern. However the case might be, the teacher would be trespassing upon the religious beliefs of quite a few students. How a teacher could with complete and cold objectivity approach the subject of the Reformation in her history class without becoming entangled in the religious dispute would perplex any realist. A friend of mine, a Jewish rabbi, told me that in questions touching upon Judaism he would not be satisfied with the material being written by a Jew. He would want it presented by a Jew, for anyone else in

[22] Irwin Shaver, *International Journal of Religious Education*, June 16, 1952, p. 13.
[23] Frank J. Sorauf, *op. cit.*, p. 788.

the very tone of his voice or misplaced emphasis might convey a wrong impression. I once asked a young junior-high student what period in history he was studying and he replied he was studying the Middle Ages, "which," so he said, "were the dark ages when people fought all the time and were sunk in superstition." Allowing for the short cuts which the young will take in answers of this kind, I could not but reflect on the affront to Catholics which this reply conveyed. I wondered what this student's teacher could have said to give this obviously incorrect historical impression. There is scarcely a field of human relations in which religion does not emerge; it can be brushed aside, which will give the impression that the matter is of no importance; it may be talked *about* with every intention on the part of the teacher of being fair, but, for most people, to hide one's feelings about religious commitments does not come easy. Objectivity becomes even more difficult if controversy surrounds a religious question of the present or the past.

Is reading the Bible in public schools a religious act prohibited by the First or Fourteenth Amendment? The reading of the Bible in public schools has frequently been challenged in the state courts and once in the Supreme Court. No clear-cut statement on the question can be derived from the decisions. Most of the decisions have upheld the reading from Scriptures if objecting students are excused or if the passages are taken from portions which Christians and Jews accept. Strangely enough, many of these decisions hold that the Bible is nonsectarian. Later cases, however, have held that the Bible is sectarian and its reading not permissible. The one Supreme Court case involving a New Jersey statute which permitted a few verses from the Bible to be read in the public schools threw no light upon the legality of the practice from the point of view of the United States Constitution.[24] The mother of a child in a public school brought the action, but the child had graduated before the Supreme Court got to the case. The Court simply held, without passing on the statute, that the mother *as taxpayer* no longer had sufficient interest in the case to bring suit. A taxpayer always has to show a *direct,* not an *indirect,* interest in a case before

[24] *Doremus* v. *Board of Education,* 342, US 429, 1952.

his standing to bring the suit will be considered by the Supreme Court. This has undoubtedly reduced the number of suits.

The question of whether or not religion may be taught at the state colleges or universities does not seem to meet with the same prohibitions which affect the grade and high schools. Certain limitations are involved it is true. State institutions of higher learning may not make discriminations among students on a basis of religious belief. Adherence to a creed may not be used as a basis for admission. Students may not be compelled to attend religious services. Even as firm an adherent of the strict form of interpretation of the separation doctrine as Professor Leo Pfeffer says: "It would seem therefore that tax-supported colleges may constitutionally provide for the objective study of religious institutions, practices, and principles. Such study must obviously be multisectarian and non-devotional. . . ."[25]

Accordingly schools of religion operate at some state universities, students are given credits for attending classes in religion, the teachers in these classes frequently are members of the various religious groups, but are paid by these groups. Catholic teachers give instruction in various phases of Catholicism, Protestant and Jewish teachers teach according to their creeds. This would appear to be an acceptable practice. Professor Sutherland comments on this practice as follows: "Religious content may well be legally tolerable in college teaching where it would not be in the fifth grade. . . . To a certain extent constitutional limitations follow popular sentiment; one seems to sense an opinion that the objectionable characteristics of religious manipulation in public education diminishes in inverse relation to the increase in intellectual resistance of the maturing student. It may be tolerated, that is to say, provided it is ineffectual and therefore awakens no resentment,—tolerance and indifference being first cousins whose relationship is often decorously ignored."[26]

How mature the average freshman or sophomore is at this stage in life when doubts and difficulties arising from emotional crisis beset him may be open to question. This, however, may be the time when he needs religious instruction and guidance more than

[25] Leo Pfeffer, *Church, State, and Freedom* (Boston: Beacon Press, 1933), p. 423.
[26] Arthur Sutherland, *op. cit.*, p. 40.

at any time in his life. An increasing number of people feel that for education to be complete, religion as an intellectual discipline may not be ignored in higher education. The Religious Education Association of the United States and Canada, composed of Catholics, Jews, and Protestants, has been in the forefront of bringing this necessity to the attention of educators and others alike. A kind of nineteenth-century pseudo-intellectualism, a kind of cultural lag, has largely been responsible for ignoring the need.

The federal government has spent millions through the so-called G.I. Bill of Rights in sending young men through both public and religious-affiliated colleges and universities. It has recently provided student loans for use in any institution. This has evidently met with public approval and no constitutional test has come before the Supreme Court.

Despite all constitutional decisions on religion and education, no one seems to be entirely satisfied with the existing situation. Extreme separationists complain about the celebration of religious holidays such as Christmas, moderate separationists are disturbed by the lack of all religion in the public schools, and upholders of the parochial school system feel that a rank injustice is done in compelling people to pay heavily for the exercise of a right. The court decisions on the separation of church and state reveal a confusion which but reflects the thinking of large numbers of people.

At this point it is well to look at suggested solutions put forward by two students of the law at the University of Chicago Law School, Professor Wilbur Katz and Professor Philip Kurland. Professor Katz believes that the central idea of the First Amendment is the protection of religious liberty. He holds that the Amendment prohibits state support of religion and confines the state to a secular activity, but that it does not restrain religious freedom. In fact, state action to *preserve* religious freedom would seem to be required by the First Amendment. Nonaction on the part of the state may in some cases result in a denial of religious liberty. Such would be the case when the state takes under its jurisdiction the lives and activities of a group of citizens. When the state takes citizens for the armed services, or runs institutions such as prisons, hospitals, or government communities leaving little opportunity for private action or support, religious liberty is denied unless provision is made for its exercise. Education may well become a government monopoly because of its cost. Therefore, if schools may not be privately maintained and their standards kept up and if secular education is the only kind afforded as an alternative, then religious liberty is denied to those who wish a religious education for their children. If the private schools could operate without great expense, then the state would do no more than to provide the liberty and protection for their existence. Or if the expense of conducting private schools were moderately heavy, then the state should make provision for released time for religious training in the public schools. However, under the present-day staggering cost of running schools, this theory would permit of assistance to private schools in the form of tuition aid, tax relief for the parents of children in private schools, or salary payments, in whole or in part, to teachers.

Professor Kurland's solution follows the nonpreferential line. He would hold that the state may not confer benefits or impose burdens on grounds of religion. It may, however, confer benefits on the basis of broad, general classifications—such as all private schools, all private hospitals, and all nonincome enterprise. The First Amendment as now interpreted has the effect of discriminating among groups; his interpretation seeks to prevent this. The Kurland theory runs athwart Mr. Justice Black's decision in the Everson case, but the Supreme Court is not bound by precedent.

At this point it is well to remember that religious-affiliated schools are not the only schools struggling with mounting costs. All private schools are affected.

One of the great inheritances of the United States is its strong system of private education. Nothing so attests to the values we place on our pluralistic culture than the support that has been given to private education, particularly on the higher level. But public education is giving our private schools a competition which in some cases is destructive. Higher salaries for teachers, lower costs for students, publicly erected and supported plant and equipment are giving public education a wide advantage over the private schools. Very valuable small private

schools face a most uncertain future. Various means of over-
coming these difficulties are being tried but the problem is far
from solved. One already hears strong voices for some kind of
government aid. Already the federal government has entered the
field by providing student loans and scholarships; this may be
by far the safest solution.

Catholics are not unaware of dangers lurking in any form of
government assistance to private education. While anxious to
avoid these dangers, they believe that some kinds of assistance
which will preserve the independence of the schools are possible.
There should be a solution to this particular phase of our school
problem which reasonable men in a frank exchange of views can
agree upon. No group in our American society should be made to
feel that oppression born of unjustified fear or prejudice weighs
heavy upon it. To the lasting credit of America it should be said
that in this country we respect the firmly held honest convictions
of our fellow citizens, but we should not require them unneces-
sarily to be martyrs to their beliefs. Every western democracy,
with the exception of the United States, regards aid to religious
schools as a provision for the common good. Can it be that in the
United States a slogan has captured our imaginations and has
prevented us from solving a problem that can readily be solved
in the interest of justice and the general welfare?

Perhaps from the point of view of law it were better to start
all over again and to have a new look at our needs and at the
intention of the law. Freedom for the believers wanes and freedom for the unbelievers grows.

Chief Justice Marshall once said that the power to tax involves
the power to destroy. There are some people unfortunately who
would desire to use the power against Catholic Church and
school property for this reason. Certain Masonic groups on the
West Coast have had this purpose in mind when they have attempted to put through by referendum process legislation taxing
schools and church property. We should, however, be clear in
our minds that other reasons exist. The problem of added sources
of revenue for our cities and states has become a serious problem
since World War I. The cities particularly have seen the most
fruitful tax sources monopolized by the federal government and
the state. The personal and real property taxes have become the

main source of revenue for local governments. Yet the burden of the property tax has become so great in many cities that the cry has been raised for added sources of taxation and for the taxation of certain properties heretofore exempt. From the very inception of our government, charitable, educational, and religious property has been exempt from taxation. In recent years the question of how much property owned by institutions of this nature should be exempt from taxation has been raised. This question has been raised not only in connection with the property of religious institutions but also in connection with the property of educational institutions. Should a large private secular university, for instance, be exempt from taxation on large real-estate holdings not devoted specifically to education or on profitable business operations? Some universities enjoy an over-all exemption of this kind by the provisions of their charters. Certain scandalous operations have been uncovered accompanying this privilege. Private parties have been known theoretically to transfer their property to such institutions to escape taxation, but with the tacit agreement that the income will be spilt between the original owner and the university. Vast business operations of religious groups—Protestant and Catholic—have been carried on free of taxation. A situation of this kind is bound to be explosive. Courts have begun to tighten up on these exemptions. In Pennsylvania only recently (December 1959) the Supreme Court of that state denied the claim of two Christian Science churches that they were entitled to tax exemption for their adjacent parking lots. The Court said that this was not a religious use. The federal government not so long ago decided that the Christian Brothers in California should pay taxes on the income from their wine and liquor business. The handwriting on the wall needs to be read by all charitable, educational, and religious institutions. No general movement exists at present for the taxation of the churches themselves, their parish houses, or the parochial and private schools, but here and there one hears the complaint that this amounts to a subsidy to religion and that people of no faith have to bear the burdens with others. The California Supreme Court upheld tax exemption for church property on the basis of the Zorach decision. A more general principle of taxation might also have been cited, that taxation need not have any direct relation to benefit. Thus if a person lives in a large city where there are several public parks, he may not claim he gets no benefit of his taxes because he never uses the parks.

Sunday closing laws are now under attack from people of no religious faith and from people who hold non-Christian faiths. A case which is coming up from one of the lower federal courts in Massachusetts and which will eventually arrive at the United States Supreme Court will test a state law which curtails commercial activity on "the Lord's Day." The question will be asked whether this is not an infringement of the rights of those who celebrate another Sabbath. Up to this time the courts have avoided the religious side of Sunday closing laws by pointing out the right of the legislature to set apart one day a week for rest from labor in the interest of the health and general welfare of the people. It is likely that the Supreme Court will follow the general line of decisions on this matter. That the selection of Sunday involves hardship on Jewish merchants should not be lightly overlooked. More devout Jews will not or cannot because of their convictions operate their places of business on Saturdays. Some who are able to do so employ Christians to work for them on Saturdays. A law providing that a person be permitted to select the day on which he would close his place of business might vitiate the whole purpose of the law. It may be safely said that the American community favors a closing law for one of the seven days of the week and by custom it favors Sunday as the day; with that hard fact before us it can only be said that Christians at least must try to make whatever accommodations are feasible for those outside of the Christian community. The difficulties and objections of the latter should not be brusquely set aside by Christians who adopt a crusading spirit for Sunday closing laws.

Censorship laws of one kind or another have always been with us. We have as a people a difficult time living with them and we would have a more difficult time living without them. While Protestants have condemned certain types of movies and in no sense favor "the sky is the limit" attitude of secularists, they have fallen into a position of suspicion of Catholic efforts to curb obscenity in all its forms. In another chapter the interfaith implications of this matter are considered. Viewing the matter here from the church-state point of view it should be kept in mind that the laws throughout the land deal with the basic offenses against the moral code purely from the standpoint of the needs of a peaceful, orderly society—standards which Catholics would call the natural law. No court has ever upheld the principle under the aegis of freedom of speech and of the press that "anything goes." Judicially it is understood that the exercise of a civil right depends upon the end that is sought. Except in times of national emergency or war the courts have tended to lean backward in applying constitutional guarantees, and even in wartime the Supreme Court has told us they lose nothing of their force. Wartime sedition acts, however, seem to contradict this point of view.

Contradictory decisions on censorship laws at the present time give us little or no basis for drawing from them a general principle. At times it appears as if the courts adhere to a purely realistic point of view on laws regarding morals; at other times it seems as if they know something must be done but that no one has discovered the right way of doing it. Some of the court decisions should command our respect for the efforts found in them to protect basic civil liberties, and there are some people so concerned about the filth abroad in the land—also a healthy concern—that they lose sight of the fact that a grave problem exists which is not settled by hasty decisions and comprehensive laws.

Aside from the problem of protecting the morals of the community, particularly of the young, we have two problems governmentally speaking. The first problem involves the enforceability or workability of a law. In the case of censorship the law must be general and its enforcement left to administrative agencies. In Europe legislation is drawn in most general terms usually, and a great deal is left to the discretion of administrative officers. In this country we have never overcome a fear and distrust of administration. In part this is due to a feeling that political patronage and general inefficiency run through all public officialdom—particularly in the states and the cities. As a consequence, it is thought, the intelligence level does not run very high. This attitude, no matter how erroneous, still prevails. In part it is due to a general reluctance to place in the hands of administrative officials, who are not directly responsible to the public, the determination of where and how precious civil rights will be exercised. Nor must it be forgotten that some stupid decisions have come from official censors.

The other problem involves the more difficult question of the respective domains of art and prudence. I doubt if our legislatures or judges think of the problems in these terms. I do not mean to say that many of the paperback productions on the newsstands or some of the productions on stage and screen represent art forms in any sense of the term, but that there are art forms which may offend some and in some cases may not be prudently offered for general use or display. The concern of the artist is not with ethics or morals. He has his own norms according to his discipline; norms which to him aim at producing good art. But art, as well as economics and general social activities, are subject to politics. In the natural order politics is the primary discipline. It deals with the important subject of the common good, or the general welfare. It must pass very difficult judgments on the best means for the attainment of the common good. Prudence is the guiding virtue of the statesman, and he may overrule the display of even a good work of art in the interest of the common good. He should, of course, have some sense of the value of art, but the artist too should have some sense of the heavy burden laid on the states-man. It is true these are general statements and most people would agree with them, but they are not self-enacting. Basic as they are, they require application to the vagaries of modern life.

The problem of censorship is further complicated by the changes in attitudes toward certain activities, modes of dress, manners of speech, and so forth. In 1890 the appearance of a young lady in a modern bathing suit would have called for police action by unanimous consent. The ultra-frank, realistic novel of today would never have passed a censor in 1900. Even the conversation indulged in today on the intricacies of childbirth would not have been mentioned beyond a whisper fifty years ago.

Faced with the "get-rich-quick" productions of smart peddlers and the intricate problems of dealing with obscenity and indecency by law, no easy answer comes to mind. The situation, however, does not mean that we are all helpless in the face of an undoubted danger to society and that the easy answer of some libertarians that nothing can be done takes care of everything.

During the Roosevelt and Truman administrations Myron Taylor, an Episcopalian, acted as personal representative of the President to Pope Pius XII. Official representation had been assigned to the Holy See from the United States twice before in our history, but no representative had been assigned since the fall of Rome to the troops of the Italian government in 1870. No great opposition to this early practice is evident. In recent years opposition of Protestant groups to any representation at the Holy See has been loud and vigorous on the ground that it violated the principle of separation of church and state. The opposition became most pronounced when President Truman sent up to the Senate the name of General Mark Clark, an Episcopalian, for approval as Ambassador to the Holy See. The resulting furor led to the General's withdrawing his name and the dropping of the proposal. Whether General Clark was to be accredited to a political or religious sovereign or both was not made clear. No court decisions may guide us as to the legality of this proposed move. We know that the President has great powers in the field of foreign affairs. He alone represents the United States in the conduct of foreign policy, and he may delegate others to act for him, always, of course, subject to the appropriation of the necessary funds by the Congress. He may break off diplomatic relations when he thinks there is sufficient cause or withhold diplomatic recognition. His appointments of ministers and ambassadors are subject to Senate approval. He may, however, at any time send personal representatives without Senate approval. Myron Taylor took care of his own expenses. It is also true that the United States may do by treaty or executive agreement what is often forbidden by the Constitution in local affairs. Aside from the fact of whether the Senate would approve such a treaty, the President could enter into a treaty with the Holy See as a foreign power. Quite likely the Senate would not approve of such a treaty, and quite likely the President would not enter into such negotiations. From the point of view of constitutional power there would seem to be no reason why the United States could not have an official representative at the Holy See. The fact that the head of Vatican City is also the head of a church should not figure, for the queen of England, and the kings of the Scandinavian countries are also heads of their respective churches. So great is the power of the President in foreign affairs there would seem to be no legal obstacle to his sending a representative to the pope as head of the Catholic Church *if* the United States interests required such representation. Far from giving the Catholic Church a position of privilege in the United States, it would furnish all groups, Catholic and non-Catholic, with a pipe-line to the head of a powerful world organization, which is now lacking. Even Bishop Pike or Bishop Oxnam would find that they as citizens of the United States could send their worries and complaints direct to the pope. To this day many specialists in foreign relations and not a few leading Protestants and Jews do not understand why there was such a furor about the matter. To most Catholics, clerical and lay, it is not a matter of great import. The Catholic hierarchy in the United States, despite unfounded accusation to the contrary, had nothing to do with the proposal. As a matter of fact reports out of Washington at the time of the controversy indicated that both Roosevelt and Truman wanted to sidestep the hierarchy by appointing their own representative.

The issue of birth control has more recently aroused the American public. As a question of church and state it has been asked whether the law can in any way buttress a belief for which the Catholic Church has become almost the sole champion. As has already been pointed out just two states, Massachusetts and Connecticut, have restrictive laws on the giving of contraceptive information.

In a recent Connecticut case before the state Supreme Court, the birth-control legislation of the state was upheld. The complainant in the case, Dr. C. Lee Buxton, of the Yale Medical School, contended that he felt professionally obligated to give his patients advice on contraception. He contended that in the case of one patient further conception meant death and in the case of others the mother would give birth to stillborn or handicapped children. The Court turned down the doctor's plea. It is presumed the case will go on appeal to the Supreme Court of the United States.

Another case involving the Connecticut statute is now in the courts of Connecticut. The plaintiffs are three Protestant clergymen of New Haven who claim that they are prevented from counseling their parishioners on family planning and that they are denied the right to carry out an obligation. The ministers are using the First Amendment to uphold their case, claiming that the state is engaged in establishing a religion by forcing the tenets of one religious group upon the whole state. We are promised other litigation, on the basis of the Fourteenth Amendment, to prove that legislation such as we find in Massachusetts and Connecticut denies equal protection of the laws. The decision of the United States Supreme Court will be awaited with interest in these cases. The painful thing for Catholics in such cases is that they have been deserted by Christians and Jews who were formerly their allies. Catholics may be driven back to the principle that the positive law cannot enforce on an unwilling community an otherwise salutary prohibition.

CHAPTER V

Non-Catholic Fears and Resentments

In recent years no group has been more carefully scrutinized, analyzed, and publicly discussed than the Catholic. In a democratic order this is as it should be. That we are maturing as a nation is indicated by the number of reasonable and honestly concerned critics of Catholicism among non-Catholics,[1] and by the serious reception of such criticisms by Catholics. In 1928, when Charles Marshall brought forward a list of objections to a Catholic's becoming President of the United States, Al Smith could honestly reply that despite his long years in public life he had never heard of such things. Today no intelligent Catholic, whether office-holder or not, is unaware of non-Catholic fears. He is often amazed at their intensity, for as he goes about the performance of his religious obligations, he gets a contrary picture to that presented to him by non-Catholic neighbors.

Why this fear of the Catholic Church, thousands of whose sons have helped to build this land, thousands of whose sons faithfully serve this land in public office, and many thousands of whose sons have died for this land? The fear extends from intelligent Protestants of good will to the hysterical fanatic filled with hatred of everything that bears the name of Rome. Dislike of some things that Catholics hold in their belief might be expected. Most Catholics, however, practicing their faith and going about their daily tasks fail to understand what all the fuss is about. The average Catholic simply knows that no one, bishop, priest, or fellow Catholic, has ever asked or required him to do anything now or for the future which would diminish his loyalty to his country. He knows that prejudice exists

[1] See the recent work published under Catholic auspices *American Catholics —A Protestant and Jewish View* (New York: Sheed & Ward, 1959).

against him and unfortunately he has been from time to time the victim of emotional spite, but he holds no bitterness because of occasional displays of injustice. He is not uncritical of his fellow Catholics, be they priests or laymen, when he thinks criticism is their due. He is fully aware that Christ gave the care of his Church in this world to men, not to angels.

To the Catholic his Church is not a power structure engaged in devious intrigues and conspicuous for the subversion of the American way of life. To him this is a caricature of something very sacred to him. As Rabbi Arthur Gilbert says: ". . . The 'power' inherent in the Catholic Church does not necessarily derive from Pope or priest. It springs rather from the commitment freely given in conscience by the many loyal Catholics whose lives and thoughts are shaped by their religious devotion and informed by the constructive influence of the liturgical life. The intensity of conviction demonstrated by Catholics who have been inspired by their faith happily dramatizes the significance that religion really can have in the lives of individuals. . . ."[2]

The very organization of the Church, however, has created deep fears and suspicion among many non-Catholics. A common belief stated by one eminent Protestant is that the Church is a huge monolithic structure that imposes everything a Catholic believes or acts upon. "In its crudest form, this image of the Church suggests that the hierarchy has a uniform opinion on absolutely everything and that the laity believe and do whatever the hierarchy tells them to believe about everything. Every Catholic is a part of this structure, usually called 'a power structure,' and will in no way deviate from what he is told to do." And he continues: "It is important, therefore, for informed Catholics and Protestants alike to help combat the prevalent notion of the completely monolithic structure of American Catholicism."[3]

Needless to say, Catholics do not view their Church as a burdensome, crushing monolith, even if it appears this way to the outsider. It is often viewed by the non-Catholic as a perfectly functioning piece of machinery that can be set in motion,

---

[2] *American Catholics, op. cit.,* p. 174.
[3] Robert McAfee Brown in *American Catholics, op. cit.,* p. 81.

either at its upper or lower reaches, by the press of a button or the simple command of a hierocrat. This is, of course, the typical American view of any administration set-up, arising from our own experiences with industrial organizations and monopolies. With our love of efficiency this is the way we would have organizations function. Organizations inspired by the Latin tradition function leisurely and, quite likely we would say, inefficiently. In any case, the American non-Catholic faced with the Catholic Church structure, headed by an absolute spiritual monarch residing in a foreign country, is left with an uncomfortable feeling that an alien leviathan controls the lives of millions of Americans. The two terms *authoritarian,* which the Church is, and *monarchy* create unpleasant images in the American mind. While the American non-Catholic prays, "Thy kingdom come" and hopefuly looks forward to the coming of a monarchy hereafter, he prefers democracy here and now. Some Americans have an exaggerated faith in what the democratic political order can accomplish and to which activities of life it may be applied. Our morals cannot be determined by the Gallup Poll, the Kinsey Reports, or even by majority vote. Our lives are controlled in scores of authoritarian ways—particularly our economic lives. A family run on democratic principles would produce incorrigible offspring. A university run by its students, even, heaven forbid, by its faculty, would disintegrate before it could educate. Democracy, an excellent political system for a people politically mature, does not fit all institutions.

Non-Catholics, however, are apt to fear this structure because within it democracy does not function as they would have it. The picture of the Church which they get from the outside is a perfect image of the operation of an ecclesiastical tyranny. Catholics have no fondness for ecclesiastical tyranny. They know that it can be the most suffocating kind of tyranny. Both Catholic and Protestant lands have known it, Catholics have seen the devastation to their Church which a justified anti-clericalism has wrought at various periods of history. American Catholics, however, have not experienced excessive clericalism.

The prestige which the Catholic clergy in America enjoys is in no small measure due to their sense of responsibility and their oneness with their people. To the American Catholic there

exists no such insidious force as the "hierarchy," particularly
as conceived by some non-Catholics. It is nothing short of amus-
ing for the intelligent Catholic to read stories saying the hierarchy
does this, or commands that, or is scheming to accomplish the
other thing. The hierarchy, that is the bishops and the arch-
bishops, meet about once a year and give the world a message
for anyone to see. These men are neither all alike nor are they
automatons with someone from afar manipulating them with
strings. In fact, unanimity among them in social and political
affairs is rare indeed. Some of them are noted for administrative
efficiency, some for a lack of it, some are friendly, some are
reserved, some are scholars, some make no pretense of scholarship; but of all it may be said that they have a keen sense of the
moods, the feelings, and the needs of the flocks under their care.
No politician operating in the democratic order could have a
better knowledge of the attitude of his constituents. Viewed
from within, this power structure contains nothing in the way of
a threat to our American system nor is it an imponderable weight
upon the shoulders of the practicing Catholics. When the hierarchy speaks, it speaks with a tone of reasoned authority, but
no one within the Church trembles or cringes in fear. And it is an
insult to intelligent Catholics for anyone to tell them they are
dupes of a devious priestcraft or unwitting agents of a conspiracy.

The idea of the efficiency of the system can also be over-
estimated. A few years ago I read in a respected Protestant
magazine a series of articles on the Catholic Church in the
United States. One article dealt with the National Catholic
Welfare Conference in Washington. This organization operates
many Catholic activities under the direction of the bishops. In
the article in question one read of a perfectly functioning organization. For instance, a priest is sent in to organize a parish,
the N.C.W.C. takes care of all his needs; they help build his
church, they furnish it, they help form the church organizations
and perhaps within a matter of a few months the parish is a going
concern. N.C.W.C. is an estimable organization and considering
its meager resources it does its work well, but even its most
ardent admirer would not boast of such efficiency as the article
pictured. It is well-nigh impossible to estimate the motives,

manner of working, and efficiency of any organization from the outside. The writer, familiar as he is with political organizations both from within and from without, often marvels that any of them are successful, considering the pulls and tensions that exist within them. Yet to the outsider they appear to be impregnable fortresses.

The Catholic Church organization is obviously composed of human beings. At one time in America the bishops were for the most part foreign born—mainly Irish. In fact, it was jokingly remarked many years ago that evidently a priest's orders were not valid unless he had been born in Ireland. Today practically all of the bishops are American born. They do not come from homes of luxury. Their parents generally have had to make great sacrifices to support them. They were reared in an American environment—they enjoyed the sports that all American boys enjoyed. They ate the same extracurricular diet of hot dogs and hamburgers, and drank cokes the same as other American youngsters. They learned to admire and cherish the memories of great heroes of American history and the great traditions of this country. They are poor stuff out of which to form a great conspiracy for subverting American life and liberties. Yet these are the men of the American hierarchy, "the minions of Rome," who according to some poor misinformed souls conspire from morning to night to control our social and political life.

The bishop is the spiritual ruler of his diocese. He is not popularly elected, for which most Catholics are quite thankful. Were a study to be made of the various episcopal jurisdictions in this country, an amazing diversity would be found. The supposed uniformity in the rule and direction of the Church throughout the country would promptly vanish if one took the time to inspect it. Let us take the matter of education. No central body controls this vast system. Many religious orders run schools and colleges and in some places these schools are in competition. Only one educational institution in the country is supervised by the hierarchy as a whole and that is the Catholic University of America in Washington, D. C. The primary schools, the high schools, and a few colleges are under the control of each diocese. Under no circumstances could a sweeping reform of the whole system, if reform were necessary, be effected. Great financial savings and, quite likely, great efficiency would result from the merging of certain institutions of higher learning within the same area, but this is no more easily accomplished than the merging of secular schools under the same circumstances.

Many other matters outside of the field of education could be cited to show the lack of centralization both in this country and throughout the world: There exist in this country several rites, each with its own liturgy performed in other languages than Latin; frequently having a married clergy; and having their own bishops. Long ago Pope St. Pius issued a *Motu Proprio* for the reform of Church music, and yet many congregations still sing hymns put to the tunes of old barroom ballads and rarely hear a Gregorian chant. But the Church gains some of its wisdom from the Roman Empire in which it was born, for neither republican nor imperial Rome interfered with the local customs in the vast regions under control. A student of administration would find the Catholic Church a most interesting object of study, for here is a world-wide organization insistent on the maintenance of basic beliefs but exercising a broad tolerance of local customs and traditions. The central government at Rome could speak with great authority on many things, but seldom does. If closely observed in practice, it is not the great monolith that its enemies maintain.

I have said that the effectiveness of the priests in this country is in large measure due to the respect which the laymen have for them. Historically this may, too, be in a measure due to Irish tradition, in which the priests were at one with their people during the tragic history of Ireland. By and large the respect of the people springs from the knowledge that the American priest serves his people well. One generally finds the clerical scholar among the order priests, parish priests furnish few scholars. Parish priests will tell you it does them little good to know the difficult problems of exegesis or the commentaries on the *Summa Theologica* when they are racing up to the fifth floor of a tenement building to bring the last rites and final consolation to a dying man. The organization of parish societies, the financial care of the parish, the care of the poor, the visiting of the sick, and the counseling of the bewildered, besides masses, funerals, and weddings do not leave much time for studious pursuits. Because of these numerous activities Catholics often listen to the worst sermons in the world. They are not at all improved by set topics sent out weekly from the chancery office of the diocese.

Not alone do the day-to-day activities of the parish priest prevent his being a studious person; they also leave little time for outside community activities. Despite the conviction of non-Catholics that the Church and its clergy mix in politics, it should be asserted that little if any of the political is heard from the Catholic pulpit, and priests stand aloof from politics, be they local or otherwise, in a way that often constitutes a fault. They express no choice of candidates for office. Community movements of political reform find the names of ministers or rabbis endorsing lists of candidates, their churches and synagogues used for meetings, and their presence at political rallies. Whatever exception there may be, it may be set down as a general rule that priests do not participate in political affairs. In drives and crusades of a social nature they may be active, the most notable kind being campaigns against indecent movies or literature. Occasionally their activity in these matters is not governed by a sense of prudence, however worthy the aim. On the whole, bishops are most sensitive on the point of their priests having any part in politics.

This is not the attitude of the bishops alone. The Catholic lay people are opposed in an extraordinary degree to political activities on the part of their clergy. They even detect a political opinion in a sermon when no such opinion is given or intended. If before our elections a bishop instructs his pastors to call the attention of their parishioners to the high obligation of voting, even this may be resented by some Catholics as favoring that political party which needs a large vote to win. During the presidential campaign of 1928 when Al Smith was the Democratic candidate and his religion was an issue in the campaign, no Catholic from one end of the land to the other heard a word from the pulpit on the burning issue of that campaign or in answer to the fantastic charges against the Catholic candidate. It can be safely asserted that non-Catholic clergymen are not so muted as the Catholic clergy in the field of politics.

The very suspicious critic of the Catholic Church will answer to all this that somehow or other the priest gives his political order to his flock in secret. No charge against the Church is more lacking in substance than this. However great the Catholic layman's respect for his clergy is, if anything of this nature were attempted the reaction on the part of the laymen would be one of extreme resentment. It may be said by some critics of the Church that they have evidence that this was done. In such a case I should first want concrete evidence and even if the evidence were given I could assert from long experience that it was indeed a rare case. I have even read one Protestant writer who boldly asserted that the political influence of the Church was exercised through the confessional. There is not a Catholic who would not assert that this is a most ridiculous charge running counter to the experience of every Catholic. The time of a priest in most urban parishes, particularly in confession, is precious. The long line of penitents waiting to be heard gives him little time for indulging in lectures on the social sciences. For the penitent the rule is as one writer succinctly put it, "Be brief, be contrite, be gone." I can think of only one remedy for a person suspicious of the church on this score—let him enter a confessional.

What I am saying applies particularly to the American clergy. The European clergy have special problems. In those countries afflicted with a serious Communist problem the Church unfortunately must enter the political field. This also applies in countries where left-wing anticlericalism is strong. In the case of the areas where communism is strong, not only is the Catholic Church being attacked, but all people holding firmly to the fundamental beliefs of the Judaeo-Christian heritage are the targets of a crusading atheism. In such cases the Church must use the only weapons she possesses—instruction and exclusion. Nor will she discourage her sons from organizing politically in self-defense. It is difficult to see how within reason any critic of the Church could object to such measures.

The increasing importance of the laity in the Church throughout the world affords a healthy antidote to the clericalism which marred the history of the Church in other times. This phenomenon, which will be discussed later (See Chapter VI), has seen the increase of laymen in the mission fields, the movement to revive the lower orders of the clerical life, the effort to foster greater lay participation in the services of the Church, and the development of the secular institutes composed of lay people to carry on the work of apostolic endeavor. The priesthood of the laity has come to have a meaning of real significance. The monolith does not function as some non-Catholics hold. The Catholic Church is a power structure indeed, but primarily a structure of vast spiritual power in which all the faithful have a feeling of participation.

Non-Catholics frequently are troubled by the authority of the pope in matters of faith or morals and the obedience of Catholics to that authority on matters touching internal politics. The confusion in the minds of people outside of the Church is understandable. Social problems do have a bearing upon morals, and to St. Thomas, ethics is not separated by a wide gap from politics. An Aristotelian might say that politics is ethics writ large. No one has any doubt when the pope speaks ex cathedra in the usually accepted sense, say in defining a dogma. An occasion of this kind is rare and surrounded with such a formality that no one can doubt the binding nature of the teaching. There are other times when he speaks through encyclicals or allocutions when he refers to teachings of long standing that are accepted. But encyclicals and allocutions may have an effect bound by time and special circumstances. Sometimes they are addressed to one nation, one group of people, or to a special issue of a particular time. The confused state of political theory in the nineteenth century in Europe brought forth many such papal statements; the famous *Syllabus of Errors* of Pius IX affords one of the best examples of such temporal statements. Sometimes the particular movement condemned changes its attitudes. For instance, socialism was generally condemned for its materialism and its general hostility to religion. Now, however, Catholics may and do belong to the British Labor Party, which is essentially the Socialist Party of Great Britain. In this country it is not unlikely that a Catholic could in clear conscience be a follower of the Norman Thomas brand of socialism.

Some encyclicals are universal in their application and the late Pope Pius XII warned that they may not be taken lightly. They constitute teachings of the Head of the Church and, while the usual formalities which surround the defining of a dogma are not present, they are binding. It is at this point that the work of the theologians begins—not always with a clarifying result for others when they have finished. The theologians expound the teaching and determine its application; it is at this point that disagreement arises and it is also at this point that the non-Catholic who looks upon the Church as the great monolith where everyone thinks alike should look in upon us.

Catholics in this country have had no experience of any statement of the popes in any way undermining their loyalty to the United States. That Catholics do not approve of certain practices approved by law or social custom in this country is no indictment of their loyalty, as a few critics would have us believe. Against all charges to the contrary it should be remembered that it is and has been through the ages a firmly established teaching of the Church that one owes obedience to the duly established civil authorities. Indeed, some critics of the Church have charged that this teaching is so absolute that it leaves little room for justifiable rebellion. The Church has ever taken very seriously the statement of St. Paul that "the powers that be are ordained by God." Church authorities generally lean backward in their application of this teaching. A few examples may illustrate this. During the days of the Irish rebellion it was generally felt by many Irish patriots that the bishops were partisans of the British because of their opposition to the use of violence. Pope Pius XI warned the Catholics of Mexico that despite the wrongs under which they suffered they should not resort to violence. And it is well within the memory of many people how severely the Church was criticized in this country for not issuing a swinging long curse on Hitler and setting the Catholics free to take up arms against him. It is believed that it is better to obey and serve an unjust regime rather than to take to the uncertain path of revolution. If this is true of a manifestly unjust regime, how much more true is it of a system such as exists in America toward which Catholics have no reason whatsoever to refuse allegiance.

That Catholics hold to certain beliefs that other Americans do not accept—not on questions of the fundamentals of a democratic regime, but on questions of general policy such as education, birth control, euthanasia, sterilization, abortions, or artificial insemination—should not bring into question their loyalty to the United States. The Catholic Church does not regard national boundaries as the limits within which fundamental beliefs are accepted or not accepted. Nor can it accept a majority vote as determining on questions of morals. The Catholic believes that some of these matters may so affect the common temporal good that a wrong decision made on them may have tragic results.

That Catholics by canon law and by preference want religion to play a part in the education of their children does not make them enemies of our public schools. One might just as readily affirm that because a man prefers to send his son to Yale he is an enemy of all the other members of the Ivy League. The American ambition of a proper education for every child is not matched anywhere else in the world. The American system of education is an imposing testimony to the sincerity of this article of the American creed. No Catholic refuses to subscribe to that creed. Yet we also justly boast in America of the diversity of the kinds of education offered. We believe that this diversity is a spur to progress and that only one kind of educational system would condemn us to a deadly uniformity. Catholics have not set out to create divisiveness in American society, and it should be remembered that greater danger may lurk in the tendencies of some ultra-patriotic people to create a uniformity of belief and practice in our society that can dampen initiative and crush the rich variety of customs out of which American society has grown. Many an Americanization program has been conceived in this way and in truth it must be said that many Catholics have shown too great an enthusiasm for them. The danger in this country stems not from the diversity of educational programs and the rich variety of schools open to the parents' choice, but from the tendency to place all education under public authority with common textbooks, common teaching methods, common examining techniques, and common subject matter. In an age when we are warned of the dangers hidden in our methods of communication through advertising, radio, and television in creating a common, mediocre mass culture, we should be seriously concerned with any attempt to undermine our rich and varied educational systems. If one complaint may be raised against the Catholic educational system, it is that it moves too much with the grain rather than against it.

The law of the Church that all parents must see to it that their children get a good Catholic education (and the late Pope Pius XII warned that it must be a *good education* as well as *Catholic*) is not a leaden yoke laid upon parents in this country. Aside from the fact that the bishops in this country have been slow to apply the law rigorously in this regard, most Catholic parents today complain that the parochial schools are unable to accommodate their children. The parochial schools lack space, not pupils.

Since the belief of Catholics on matters such as artificial insemination, euthanasia, or abortion (other than therapeutic) is still pretty generally shared, one does not find any complaint against the Church. With birth control it is another matter—a question which say ten years from now may not figure at all if acceptable natural means of limiting the number of children for proper cause is found. The complaint at the present time is that Catholics seek to impose their views on this question upon an unwilling public. In the democratic process this may be inevitable. If in a referendum I vote on a proposition that impinges upon or involves morals, birth control, prohibition, gambling, boxing, or the like, and I happen to be in the majority, I am, of course, imposing my view on a minority for what I believe to be the greater good. At the same time, I should know, from what I have already said of positive law, that I should be extraordinarily prudent in voting for sumptuary law. Whatever might be said for the Catholic voters in Massachusetts and Connnecticut, it is questionable if a right that is undoubtedly theirs has been used with practical wisdom. Pressure politics both for good and for ill has become a part of our democratic process, but high pressure from a religious source does not go down well with the American public. This obvious fact needs to be underlined many times. Particularly hard to take is a pressure campaign that implies that all who disagree with us on a principle of natural law are immoral. It may well be that the Catholics of these states might ask themselves whether this is not a question on which consciences have to be educated and the force of positive law eliminated.

When the question is asked what Catholics would or should

do in the case of government promotion of artificial contraception, one moves from a matter of simple prohibition to a matter of government approval and sanction. Catholics should not be blamed for protesting that this is a grave matter of conscience for them, nor charged with cruel lack of concern for the misery and starvation of people. One unfortunate aspect of the present controversy concerning the use of government funds in foreign lands for the spread of birth-control information is that it endangers the whole worth-while program of foreign aid. It further gives strength to the argument that the United States is vitally interested in reducing the population pressure so long as people of color comprise the group to be affected. The latter assumption, of course, is not true, but its use for propaganda purposes is beyond comprehension. Even granting an urgency about the population explosion, would it not be in the interest of fairness for all concerned to pour their resources into private agencies for the solution of the problem, a method suggested by President Eisenhower? Would it not be a wiser policy to follow the general principle that government should not be called in until other available means have been tried? It would seem that even advocates of artificial contraception as a solution to overpopulation might object to riding roughshod over Catholic consciences and upsetting the good will among citizens so necessary for the stability of political order. Is this too not a problem that might find a more reasonable solution were representative Catholics and non-Catholics to sit down and talk this matter over rather than screaming at each other in the public forum?

If the law permits in most states the giving of information on birth control, I can see no other way for Catholics than the toleration of giving such information in public institutions. Sources where such information will be available will be plentiful enough and there would seem to be no reason why Catholics should be compelled in their own institutions to violate what is to them a high matter of principle. If Catholics find it very difficult to accept the diverting of their taxes for support of birth-control clinics in public institutions, it would appear to be basely inconsiderate to penalize their own institutions where birth-control information is not available.

If Catholics bow to a situation of which they do not essentially approve, as in the case of the giving of contraceptive information, it is not because a majority of people practice it, not even because statistics may show that even some Catholics practice it. Majority votes cannot make an immoral action moral for Catholics any more than it can for Protestants. They would still believe that it were better for the common good if contraception were not practiced. And they would also insist that there is no difference between the good of the person and the common good. On the other hand the acceptance of an order of things less than the perfect might be founded on the words of St. Thomas Aquinas: "The good and welfare of an associated multitude is the preservation of its unity, which is called peace, without which the utility of social life is destroyed—nay more, the discordant multitude becomes a burden to itself."[4]

While one hears less of the opposition to the Church because of its stand against therapeutic abortion, the Catholic is not allowed to forget it. The lessened outcry no doubt is due to the advance in medical science which has made the procedure less common. Even before this, however, the fear existed in some medical circles that therapeutic abortions were becoming far more frequent than some situations warranted. The tendency of lazy, incompetent, or morally blind doctors to take the easy way out in handling difficult pregnancies was a matter of concern to many Catholic and non-Catholic doctors alike. To the credit of the medical profession, however, they did not look upon the problem as a question of saving either the unborn child *or* the mother but a problem of the lives of both—which has been the view of the Catholic Church. That progress has been made in this direction has been due to the dropping of the "either/or" proposition by reasonable people.

Among some non-Catholics a complaint is raised against Catholics because of their rigorous attitude on divorce. However rigorous the attitude may be, it has not affected the wide choice of legal bases for divorce in this country, which range all the way from adultery to a passing quarrel at morning breakfast. The number of divorces granted in the United States, as well as the mounting number of cases of juvenile delinquency which have

[4] *De Regimine Principum,* Bk. I, Ch. 2.

been traced to broken homes, has aroused not only Catholics but non-Catholics as well. It is interesting to note that it was well along in the present century before one over-whelmingly Protestant state, South Carolina, granted divorces. One does not find a uniform attitude toward our divorce laws among non-Catholics. While few favor the Catholic view, many have come to see that we have not solved the grave problems of marital unhappiness by taking the easy way out of the difficulty. Catholics will undoubtedly register a protest in most states against the liberalizing of divorce laws and will favor the restricting of grounds for divorce in states where the process is scandalously easy. It is probably true that they will not seek the abolition of divorce even in states where their voting strength is great.

Catholics are not unaware of the irritation caused to non-Catholics by the firm position Catholics hold on mixed marriages. Among many Jews the attitude toward mixed marriages resembles that of the Catholic. But the Catholic rules on the subject are more definitely spelled out. Such a marriage must be performed before a Catholic priest and the children of such a marriage must be reared as Catholics. A mixed marriage is not inevitably an unhappy one, but the danger of indifference to all religion in a house built on such foundations is great. The possibility of religious dissension wrecking such a home is ever present. To the irritation of non-Catholics, Catholics insist upon the full enforcement of adoption laws which respect the wishes of the deceased parents of orphaned children in the rearing of the children in the parental faith. It would seem strange indeed that anyone should contest this sacred right and obligation of parents. To Catholics the surest way of respecting the wishes of the deceased parents in religious matters is to insist that foster parents belong to the faith in which the children are to be reared. Any other course constitutes the breaking of a sacred trust.

"Part of the difficulty in Protestant-Catholic communications lies in the different premises which are brought to the discussion. These premises can be summaried as follows: The Catholic believes not only that his Church, and his Church alone, has possession of final truth, but he further believes that his Church's *way of stating the truth* is beyond possibility of error," writes

Reverend Robert McAfee Brown of Union Theological Seminary.[5] This is a common complaint against Catholics. Many non-Catholics of good will feel that this stand of the Church makes communication difficult if not impossible. And it is understandable that the position of the Catholics inevitably causes resentment. Does this position, however, make communication impossible? In the first place there are wide areas in the field of theology where Catholic theologians do not agree and in which an official position does not exist. One glance at Catholic theological journals will convince anyone of this. Difficulties, perhaps we can say mystery, surround many a spiritual truth, but the human reason, the depths of which will never be fully ascertained, may and should be applied to them. Even Catholics whose stand is fixed on many theological matters can have the approaches to a truth clarified, or even the truth itself, by discussion. How far, however, does a definite stand by one side prevent fruitful discussion? Few there are who do not enter a conference with some fixed point of view. Discussion is impossible without some basic agreements which are fixed for both parties. Is it not obvious that all Christians hold to certain basic doctrines such as the historicity and divinity of Christ? Would, therefore, discussion with the Jews be possible? The important theological discussions now going on in Germany between Catholics and Lutherans, which have been proceeding for some years, testify to the fact that discussion is not only possible but can be exceedingly fruitful. While unquestionably the insistance of the Catholics that theirs is the one true Church and that that Church teaches with the voice of Christ Himself may irritate non-Catholics, it is my belief that if adequate communication does not exist in this country, other reasons lie behind this unfortunate situation, the blame for which can be fairly evenly distributed on both sides. Any Catholic, however, who with condescending air and with stiff-necked pride looks upon his non-Catholic brethren is ignorant of certain fundamental teachings of his own faith. If he belongs to the true Church, it is not due to any merit of his own and this should teach him humility. If he has not learned that he is

[5] *American Catholicism, op. cit.,* p. 63.

bound to all men through a common Fatherhood he is lacking in the greatest of the theological virtues, charity.

A long list of non-Catholic complaints and disagreements with Catholics in domestic affairs could be drawn up. Some of them, such as the fantastic notion that Catholics want to put the pope in the White House, can be dismissed as coming under the heading of the psychopathic. Looking, however, over several selected irritations which have stirred people locally and nationally, we might first notice the question of gambling. One American Protestant has said: "Whether bingo is the best method of raising money for a church or not, it annoys those who do their gambling through pari mutuel, the numbers racket, the New York Stock Exchange, the Irish Sweepstakes, or even the normal joyous method of free enterprise in an expense-account economy."[6] Whether this is a fair way of putting the question or not, it is true that Protestants regard all forms of gambling as morally wrong and that Catholics do not. It should be noted that this is a moral question to Protestants and that Catholics may return the charge so often thrown their way that a special group within the community is trying to impose its moral standards on the whole community. Many Catholics do have the feeling that Catholics very often go too far out in defense of gambling. Non-Catholics might even be forgiven the error of believing that somehow or other bingo is enshrined in the dogmas of the Church. Not a few Catholic as well as non-Catholic officials in public office have stated either publicly or privately that our restrictive gambling laws have given birth to more sinister rackets than is healthy for any community. It is obvious that it is difficult to enforce upon a community rules of conduct in which it does not believe. The breakdown in morale of many a police department has been due to laws of this kind. On the other hand, churches do not need bingo to exist, and some Catholics seem to put more faith in it than they do in the Holy Ghost. And Protestants should remember that their moral concern on gambling has not been traditional, for in days when this was definitely a Protestant country many a worthy enterprise was supported by a lottery, to which there was no general objection

6 Stringfellow Barr in *American Catholicism, op. cit.,* p. 9.

—note the funds that went into Harvard University by this method. As a consequence, it seems to many Catholics that the furor and opposition to gambling, particularly in the form of bingo, is as much due to the fact that Catholic churches use it as to any other cause. The whole country would benefit if Catholics and non-Catholics would sit down together and in a rational spirit consider the social effects of gambling under present laws and seek effective legislation to meet the situation. But effective legislation, it should be noted, will not be ideal legislation from one's moral point of view.

Two other areas of conflict have been discussed elsewhere, namely the appointment of an official American envoy to the Holy See and censorship (Chapter IV). No attempt will be made to enlarge on the considerations heretofore treated. Let us therefore pass on to other controversial matters. Most Americans, Catholic and non-Catholic alike, share the Catholic Church's concern on communism. There is a fear among non-Catholics that among Catholics the matter has gotten out of hand. The feeling abounds that it has become such an emotion-charged issue that Catholics have lost the ability to face it rationally. It is pointed out that Catholics in Europe, face to face with living Communist parties, do not show the same hysteria displayed by American Catholics. This anomalous situation may be explained not only by a healthy fear of communism, but also by that psychological reaction of Catholics, who are so often charged with holding a foreign allegiance that they have become more than one hundred per cent patriotic and American. No unfriendly voice puts it this way: "But the Church . . . had become so obsessed with the danger of Communism that it failed as an organized body to respond as effectively as it might to some of the other crucial social problems of our day: the preservation of individual civil liberty even as security in maintained, the creative seeking for peace through international involvement while national military strength is preserved, and a host of other issues."[7] Some Catholics well remember what a painful experience it was to question in any degree the justice of the McCarthy or Jenner precedures in discussions or talks before certain

---

[7] Rabbi Arthur Gilbert, *American Catholicism, op. cit.*, p. 177.

Catholic groups. It must be admitted that the adherence of certain Catholics to the McCarthy cause had something of the wild and untamed about it—a holy war without quarter asked or given. This was not as many non-Catholics believe because of Senator McCarthy's Catholicism, because the same enthusiasm existed in Catholic circles for the work of Congressman Dies, a non-Catholic, who initiated the drive to hunt out subversives. The valiant endeavor of the *Commonweal* and even the dispassionate approach of Rome itself could not dampen the zeal of Catholic patriots. Aside from the crusade against communism, it must be admitted in all frankness that Catholics have not shown an outstanding concern for the maintenance of civil liberties to the same degree as their non-Catholic fellow citizens. Most unfortunate of all has been the lack of concern in this area among the students at our Catholic educational institutions. Catholics have given the impression of a much greater interest in prohibitions than in fundamental guarantees of liberties.

Non-Catholics along with many Catholics regret the absence of Catholics in causes for civic improvement. In some areas it is well-nigh impossible to recruit any sufficient number of Catholics for local reform or improvement projects. For many years the absence of Catholic women from such fine civic organizations as the League of Women Voters caused not a few people to think that we talked more than other people about the common good but did little to promote it. Often Catholics will complain about some people in the leadership of such movements who are "suspected radicals" or about some one item of a program of which they do not approve. If the general aim of the movement is good it would seem to be the better part of wisdom for Catholics to join and to make their influence felt from within. In most movements of this kind we cannot expect to have a Federal Bureau of Investigation check on every person involved nor a program one-hundred-per-cent acceptable. Crusades for clean literature or morally acceptable movies are not the only possible spheres in which Catholics can and should work. Unfortunately, while improvement of the situation has been noticeable, the complaint of nonco-operation from Catholics in civic causes has yet much truth to it.

Non-Catholics frequently complain of inability to establish

any kind of effective communication with Catholics. The complaint comes especially from non-Catholic clergy who contend that communication with Catholic priests is almost impossible. More will be said of this later, but non-Catholics will have to remember that the situation they regret is partly of their own making. Priests are generally forbidden to take part in political action, but the term political has very often been so extended that it covers almost every social movement. Non-Catholics often unjustly complain of the political influence of the Catholic clergy; the latter, therefore are most careful to give no cause for the charge. Under any circumstances, however, priests will be most careful in avoiding entanglements in politics. Their parishioners would not have it otherwise, but co-operation in broad matters of social reform and the promotion of improved interfaith relations would be welcomed by people generally. The Catholic clergy have been too isolated from the clergy of other faiths and much misunderstanding has been the result.

Professor Bennett, a critic not to be taken lightly, has a further criticism to make of Catholics in this country when he says: "Non-Catholics have grounds for resenting and fearing the tendency of Roman Catholics, when they have power, to seek control of the public-school system to band it in their part to Catholic purposes. Parochial schools could operate as safety valves for the public schools, but this is not often the case. When Roman Catholics dominate the public school boards they sometimes discriminate against non-Catholic teachers. In extreme cases that have been publicized they have operated public schools as though they were parochial schools. Perhaps more serious in the long run is the tendency of Roman Catholics in some places to oppose needed bond issues or appropriations for the public schools. This is not a surprising reaction to the double burden of education costs that they themselves bear, but it is very bad for education."[8]

These are reasonable charges, but the answer to the burden of these charges must be a *tu quoque*. This excuses no one guilty of these practices. Unfortunately, it still remains true in a section of the United States that discrimination in the public school

[8] Bennett, *op. cit.*, pp. 255-56.

system favors the Protestants. One only has to take a look at the requests for teachers that fill the files of placement offices to note how badly the Catholics and Jews make out. It is not pleasant either to read the recommendation which so frequently contains the phrases "While a Jew" or "Despite the fact that he is a Catholic," etc. These recommendations are generally sent to the institutions of higher learning, public and private, almost at once cutting off the possibility of employment. This writer remembers so well the administration of the public schools in Chicago during the time of Mayor William Hale Thompson when Masonic affiliation played such a major role in teacher employment and promotion. In a recent visit to California I talked to a Methodist friend of mine who was teaching in one of the public junior colleges of that state. He told me that not long ago he had been interviewed for a teaching post by the president of a new junior college, which was to be opened in the southern part of the state. The president in the interview told him that in order "to fit into" the new college community it were better that he be a Protestant—but not a member of one of "the extreme Protestant groups." The president also suggested that my friend should be a Republican in politics. At this point, my friend tells me, he was somewhat confused. He was certain that in politics he was a Democrat, but he was not certain in his own mind about the acceptability of his Methodism.

The trouble frequently lies with the feeling among Catholics in certain areas that discrimination has for so long been exercised against them, that the situation will be righted by the employment of a large number of Catholic teachers. This is, obviously, not a proper view for anyone to take. One may understand it from a human point of view, but objectively it is wrong in that it introduces a religious spoils system into our public schools.

How about the Catholic vote on public-school bond issues? It is not easy to get voting statistics on any group, and perhaps it is true that in some places Catholics have voted against such propositions. At the same time one must remember that the tendency of the American public to favor bond issues is never enthusiastic. But to say that Catholics habitually or for the most part vote against public-school bond propositions could in no sense be justified. One only has to look around, particularly in the communities of the North, and see the rate of public-school construction to realize that no group is carrying on a filibuster against this worthy enterprise. It would be altogether unreasonable for Catholics, over fifty per cent of whose children attend public schools, to undermine the possibilities of these children receiving a decent education. It is the opinion of the author that Protestants who give credence to this charge should rely much more carefully on expertly accumulated statistics.

Protestants as such have not been in the struggle (with the exception of the militantly unfriendly PAOU) against those special areas where the parochial school is the public school. In these localities the Catholic group is so numerous that only two or three children belong to non-Catholic religious groups. Many of these areas, generally small in population, have for generations had but one school. In not a few of the cases special nationalities, particularly French or German, constitute the bulk of the population. It is not within the realm of the practical to build a large public school for a mere handful of students and a solution is found in employing bus transportation to the nearest public school if the parents of the children desire it. In some instances religion in these parochial schools is taught only during the first hour of the day. The support of the school comes from public taxes. Considering the vigor of the attack which the American Civil Liberties Union launches against these schools, one might conclude that they were the result of local conspiracies recently hatched. The building of a special public school would force upon such a community a solution uneconomic, unreasonable, impractical, and oppressive. If any one of these communities should grow in population, the non-Catholic population would increase and public schools would have to be provided. In the meantime it would seem more consonant with the American spirit to respect their local autonomy.

Professor Bennett—and I quote him because I believe him to be a sincere and responsible critic—brings a further charge against Catholics when he says: "Non-Catholics have grounds for criticizing in no uncertain terms the behavior of authorities of the Roman Catholic Church in other countries, especially Spain and some Latin American countries. . . . Whenever Ameri-

can Catholics bring pressure on their government in favor of the
Roman Catholic Church as against Protestantism in Latin American countries, American Protestants have a right to be disturbed
and to bring counter-pressures as they have done."[9]

Frankly, American Catholics are embarrassed by the handling
of religious minorities in Spain, nor do they sanction violent
treatment of non-Catholics in Latin America or anyplace else.
In this country the enthusiastic support which Catholics have
given to Generalissimo Franco has heightened the suspicion
which non-Catholics have of the American Catholic views on
Spain. Here again a difference should be noted between American Catholics and European Catholics. Few of the latter showed
the enthusiasm for the Generalissimo in the Civil War which the
former displayed. It is natural that non-Catholics should remember the all-out support that the Generalissimo received in most
Catholic circles in this country and should interpret this support as an approval of all his regime has done. While American
Catholics were swept into this position by their antagonism to
communism, they left themselves open to the charge of support-
ing a Spanish form of fascism, with all its known opposition to
civil liberty.

The Church is not so powerful in these matters as some non-
Catholics believe. Professor Brown, for instance, says: "Protestants cannot help having the feeling that if there is really something wrong with the treatment of Protestants in Spain, the
Catholic Church both could and should condemn such treatment, and that the policy could be changed literally overnight
if the Church wished it to be changed."[10] This assumption does
not take into account the traditions and customs long-engrained
in the institutions of a people. Nor does it take into account the
effect of sudden change upon the behavior of a people. Political
scientists often speak of the "Poverty of Power," and point out
the limits within which power may be exercised—especially,
short of creating revolution. While very many American Catholics would like to see Spain "open up," yet to speak of what
should be done from our American viewpoint may not be best
for Spain. Some American Catholics feel that you cannot keep

[9] Bennett, *op. cit.*, pp. 255-56.
[10] Robert McAfee Brown, *American Catholicism, op. cit.*, p. 78.

the lid fastened down on the activities of people in the modern world, even if they are historically conditioned to a lid, without building up a pressure that finally blows all established institutions to bits. The Church, however, is always conservative in its approach and will work within a nation according to the customs which that nation has built up for itself. This is a point to remember when considering whether Catholics would overturn our institutions if they had a majority to do so. Spain is an anomaly in the modern world, American Catholics do not understand it any better than American non-Catholics, and would it not be better for both to look more seriously at the problems at our doorstep and direct attention first to them? Would it not be well to let the Spaniards see that Catholics and non-Catholics in this country operating together with freedom for all groups provide the best basis for religious growth and political stability?

Arguments from history either for or against a cause provide uncertain material for controversy at best. We have worn out the decline of the Roman Empire in this way. Yet what Catholics have done in the past lies behind many fears of the non-Catholics. While most Catholic nations today practice a commendable tolerance and no Catholic nation, even the most rigorous, has any plan to establish the Inquisition with all the horrors which some people ascribe to it, there still remain the bloody specters of past ages to haunt the minds of many a sincere non-Catholic. Catholics, too, have certain memories of ages gone by when they were on the receiving-end of the persecution. The assumptions behind non-Catholic fears seem to stem from a belief that Catholics have learned nothing since the sixteenth century. Despite the fact that all respectable Catholic historians have condemned most severely the excesses of Catholics, lay or clerical, in centuries gone by, it is still believed in some quarters that we keep the rack and the screw ready to be dusted off for immediate use. Granted that this is stating a point of view in its crudest form, yet its present-day more intelligent form is that the Church stands for suppression purely and simply. The Church as a historical institution comes into our day bearing all the marks of the blessings it has wrought in the past—which are sometimes forgotten—and all the errors its leaders have been guilty of. It has a continuous history and the customs and manners of each succeeding age are marked upon it. It has carried on its mission through human beings who have been children of the times in which they lived and in perspective they do not measure up to what we demand today. Its teachings and its ideals have always been far ahead of the practices of the time, but since it operated in the world, it has had to make the most of what it found in customs of time and place. But its very longevity has been in part owing to its adaptability. Its leaders, it is true, often belied the term Christian in the cruelties they took from the current pattern of punishment and suppression. Spain to the contrary, the Church today has and will adjust itself to the new conditions of human freedom and responsibility. The impending danger of intolerance today comes not from a religious but from a political source and in that struggle the Church may be, as it has been before, the protector of man's dignity and his rights as a person. Totalitarian states do not deny her the right to exist because she appears as a rival totalitarian power, but because of her uncompromising defense of the Christian concept of man.

Many fears which non-Catholics entertain toward their Catholic fellow citizens in the United States may be grouped under the general heading of the political. What do Catholics do in politics? What are their motives? Who directs them? Are they not the source from which the political machines and the bosses are drawn?

When many years ago the waves of immigration from abroad hit these shores, particularly the influx of immigrants from Ireland, the control of American politics lay securely in the hands of native Americans, some of whom dated their ancestries back before the founding of the Republic. It may be difficult for people today to realize that even Tammany Hall in its early days was not only composed of the older stock, but that it was definitely inclined to be anti-Catholic. While the Catholic Germans moved more generally to the farms, the Irish remained in the cities. There they learned their politics from the native sons and the latter made full use of their voting power in a day when suffrage was easy to come by. Barred from positions of prestige and preferment, the Irish took the one path to wealth and recognition—politics. The native Americans filled the professional and business positions. Following the Civil War the Irish were well-entrenched in politics in most American cities. They still could not be elected to the higher posts in government, but within the political organization they assumed positions of leadership. From 1870 to 1900 the general moral tone of American business, professional, and political life hit its lowest point. The higher echelons of American society frequently made great fortunes by grand larceny and the lower ranks made smaller fortunes by petty larceny. It was not an era to be proud of. And the guilt did not follow religious lines. New York City reached its lowest depths under Tweed, who, while most considerate of the Irish rank and file, was not a Catholic. The machine leadership in most of the cities was not Catholic. This is not said to disparage non-Catholics in any way but to disabuse the minds of some people of the belief that Catholics were largely responsible for machines and machine government in our cities. Catholics did not invent the system, whatever uses they made of it in their turn. The big bosses in American political life, such as Conkling, Platt, Barnes, Hanna, Quay, and Vare were not members of the Catholic faith.

The great struggle for political reform began about 1900. Since that time political machines, while thriving for a time, have had a more difficult time holding on to power for any length of time. Our largest cities have gone through periods alternately of machine control and reform, but by and large a more alert electorate has made the reign of the corruptionist more tenuous. The type of boss or organization in an area will reflect the religious and nationalistic composition of the area. While William Hale Thompson of Chicago came of English ancestry, the leaders of his machine were largely Scandinavian, German, and Protestant. On the other hand boss Hague of Jersey City had an Irish and Catholic organization. The mistake is often made, however, of thinking that only the cities provide examples of machine control; counties, villages, and New England towns also have had their bosses and their machines. It has not been unusual on election days for rural areas to hold back the counting of votes until the large cities have reported, and then to make necessary changes in the ballots to overcome the urban vote. Or a New England town may hold down the number of new businesses in order to prevent competition with the establishments run by older families. Good government or political corruption are not the sole characteristics of any one religious or nationalistic group in the United States.

Catholics, however, resent political corruption on the part of their fellow Catholics whether the number of such bad citizens be great or small. Catholics are awake to the danger to our institutions caused by dishonesty in public office, and in recent years, as has been said, they have lost no opportunity in condemning the Catholic who runs a machine or the Catholic who profits from one. Within recent years many able public servants have come from the Catholic citizenry. An examination of the government of the states at the present time would show many able Catholic governors and, added to such a list, would be mayors and members of the Congress. The reason why these people have not been better known as Catholics is that they have neither flaunted their religious profession nor have used their offices for special favors for their Church.

What of the voting habits of Catholics? Political scientists know that the ordinary conception of bloc voting is a myth, whether one thinks of labor, the farmers, or religious groups. If any one element holds a group together, it is the tendency of nationalistic groups of fairly recent origin to combine. Groups of like-minded people may vote the same ticket in large enough numbers to swing an election one day or another, but what the whole group will do is hidden in the secrecy of the voting booth. Because the Catholic population has been for years an urban population, it has been Democratic, reflecting the views of most urbanites. In recent years, with the movement of Catholics to the suburbs, there has been a stronger trend to the Republican Party, which for various social and economic reasons more definitely represents the views of the voters in those areas. One look at the spectrum of Catholic voting would indicate at present views from the extreme right to the liberal left. Wealthy Catholics normally do not have the same voting habits as Catholics in the labor groups. A conservative Catholic who would not permit the *Commonweal* or *America* to be read in his home has little in common in his voting with the Catholic who adheres loyally to the Americans for Democratic Action. In other words, Catholics normally vote as other Americans vote, according to their economic or social views. In local and state elections where Catholic office-holding has become more commonplace, they give little or no thought to the religious affiliation of candidates. A public-opinion analyst, Elmo Roper, denies that even for a Catholic candidate would there be any sizable swing of Catholic votes to his standard because of his Catholicism. He calls attention to the wide diversity of nationalities among Catholics and concludes: "Catholics are liberals—and they are conservatives. Catholics belong to labor unions—and Catholics are unhappy about labor unions. Catholics are Republican—and they are Democratic. . . . It seems to surprise some people that Catholics are people."[11]

While many non-Catholics have lived under Catholic officials, mayors, and governors, and have even supported them, they are most hesitant to support a Catholic for the office of President of the United States. A recent poll of over seven hundred Presbyterian ministers indicated that over fifty per cent of them would not vote for a Catholic for Presidential office. The ordinary Catholic finds this difficult to comprehend and he may ascribe it to a bigotry unworthy of intelligent people. There are many non-Catholics who genuinely believe for various reasons that a Catholic President could not serve the country according to its laws and traditions. Robert Michaelson, writing in the *Christian Century* (February 3, 1960), gives us one reason for non-Catholic opposition. He says that the President has become a symbol or image of America. He represents not only what the country is, but its host of traditions and customs. These traditions the non-Catholic thinks of as Protestant. The President, if he is not a church member, is expected to join a Protestant church and to worship there with more or less regularity. The non-Catholic is not happy with the vision of a President who would go to Mass and would attend to his obligations as a Catholic. The non-Catholic's idea of what symbolizes America today may be wrong, and no doubt it would be better for all if he conceived that symbol as representing the world's greatest

[11] *Saturday Review,* October 31, 1959.

experiment of people of all faiths and nationalities living together in peace. This may be more truly the symbol of America, but traditions and inherited beliefs play as great a part in shaping the mind of the non-Catholic as they do the mind of the Catholic.

It is doubtful if any cure for the fears that afflict non-Catholics on the question of a Catholic's holding the Presidency can ever be sufficiently dispelled until there is a Catholic President. Within one month of his taking office the country will be debating whether he has cured inflation, whether his defense policies are sufficient for our protection, whether his ideas on the responsibility of government in social problems go far enough. His religious affiliation will be largely forgotten and the American public will judge him as they have judged others holding the office.

Catholics confronted with the question of a Catholic President are not of one mind. Some do not wish to go through the election year of 1928, when Governor Smith was a candidate, all over again. Others feel that a Catholic President would have to lean over backward in his actions in order to allay all suspicions. Still others fear that the first Catholic President might not measure up to ordinary standards as a good executive, not because of his Catholicism, but because of a lack of ability, that his poor performance might be associated with his religion. While Catholics will not vote as a block for a Catholic candidate for the Presidency, continued opposition from non-Catholic groups to a Catholic candidate will naturally tend to drive many Catholics into his camp.[12] Worst of all, such opposition would once again send Catholics into their ghetto, from which they have been slowly emerging. A repetition of the 1928 political battle would be little short of a disaster for Catholic–non-Catholic relations and for the internal peace of America.

It is well that Catholics consider seriously the fears which non-Catholics have and move in whatever direction they can to eliminate these fears. At the same time there is no gain if each group tries to be sweet and polite simply for the sake of avoiding argument. Mature people can be frank without hurt. There will always remain some fears and many disagreements. The

[12] Note the Wisconsin primary election of 1960.

main problem is always to maintain mutual respect and to govern our relation in a spirit of charity and understanding. Fears, challenges, and disagreements will be dangerous to the peace of America if each group remains within its enclosures and holds itself in isolation, where hysteria and wild phobias breed profusely.

CHAPTER VI

The Catholic Critique

Of all aspects of the problem of church and state in this country none is more currently in controversy than the relation of the Catholic schools to public authorities. Catholics are determined that religion shall not be divorced from education and by religion they mean the Catholic religion. Despite the increasing financial burden the determination is in no wise lessened. Yet as we have seen, the constitutions of most of the states as well as the decisions of state courts prohibit aid to parochial schools. Certain indirect aids such as school lunch programs, the furnishing of textbooks, and the transportation of parochial-school children in public buses have been approved by the United States Supreme Court. Catholic resentment against efforts of non-Catholic groups to refuse these, particularly bus transportation, has become in recent years a major obstacle to the growth of healthy interfaith relations. The logic of non-Catholic opposition to the public transportation of parochial-school children is no less clear to Catholics than it was to a Norwegian Lutheran who, when hearing of the non-Catholic position, wanted to know if Catholic school children had to pay a special tax for use of the sidewalks on the way to and from school.

Catholics also find it difficult to understand why some non-Catholic groups carry their opposition to the parochial schools to such an extent that only the deepest bigotry could motivate it. Such animosity was responsible for the recent unsuccessful effort in California to tax the parochial schools. It should be said in passing, however, that many fair-minded non-Catholics went to every effort to block the passing of the referendum.

It has already been pointed out that there lurks a danger in state aid—particularly direct aid. And Catholics are not unaware

of this. Nor do Catholics wish to see the public schools under-
mined by an extensive assistance to religious-affiliated schools.
Tuition aid to students, tax relief for the parents of children
attending the parochial schools, and even public *loans* to religious groups at relatively low rates of interest for building
purposes would seem to be practical and legally justifiable.

Has not the time arrived when this whole issue needs to be
taken out of the field of public controversy where many mis-
understandings have arisen and false issues have been injected?
One wonders what the result would be if several carefully chosen
representatives of the National Council of Churches of Christ
and an equal number of carefully selected representatives of
the National Catholic Welfare Council were to sit down together
to find a solution to this problem. Certain areas of agreement
would at once be found and might be stated as follows:

1. The public school system must be maintained at its greatest
efficiency.

2. By tradition this country is committed to the proposition
that private education may function along with public education.

3. Dependence on public funds can lead to the destruction of
private education.

4. It is, however, a function of the states to see to it that certain standards of teaching are maintained in both public and
private schools.

Such a committee could proceed to examine our own history
on the relation of the state to education and to examine the systems established in other lands with their strong and weak
points. Several sessions might be given to reports on what the
private and religious-affiliated schools are doing, and excursions
might be made to these schools to see their systems in operation.
Finally an examination should be made of the method of financing these schools to determine if the best methods are in
effect to avoid unnecessary waste. I do not suggest Jewish representation in the initial proceedings, but if some consensus is
arrived at by Catholics and Protestants, then further conferences
should be held with Jewish leaders. Opposition from outside of
the religions to any solutions agreed upon might be expected,
but at least the area of disagreement would have been limited.

In Protestant opposition to Catholics in this country one finds a great deal of the less objective features of Reformation controversy. When American Protestants "get back to the Reformation," they do not follow the course set by their European brethren of getting back to fundamental questions alone; they are apt to include, as the political scientist would say, all the campaign literature of the period. Campaign literature on any side of a controversy is untrustworthy. Like the campaign literature of a presidential campaign in this country, it is exaggerated, full of name-calling, propaganda in its worst sense, and quite often contrary to fact. As any campaign proceeds, the campaign literature becomes more and more unreliable. It cannot be denied that as the Reformation movement wore on, many rulers, prime ministers, and officials of the states involved, whether they were Catholic or Protestant, jumped into the fray with far other than religious purposes. According to the charges and countercharges, the Jesuits were always engaged in intrigues and conspiracies and the reformers were setting the people free of all moral restraints. Luther was thoroughly corrupt, according to the Catholic controversialists, and the popes were anti-Christs to followers of the Reformers. The caricatures drawn of the leaders by both sides were fantastic. It is interesting to speculate what fruitful negotiations might have been carried on had not the dust of battle precluded any vision of fundamental issues. Yet even today in some Protestant quarters the only image of Catholicism comes from the campaign literature. Within our own time some Protestant catechisms have referred to the pope as anti-Christ or the Beast of the Apocalypse. The Jesuits, the most irenic group in the Catholic Church, are still conspirators who believe that the end justifies the means. The profound questions of faith, grace, the nature of the Eucharist give place to a discussion of whether or not the pope will take over the White House and subvert all our freedoms. Could it be that in America generally our scholarship is more given to the effects of certain beliefs than to the truth of the beliefs themselves? Or are we so lacking in faith in our own democratic institutions, as has sometimes been charged, that we look for spies and saboteurs in every nook and corner?

What is the fear of Catholics behind their firm opposition to birth control, divorce, sterilization, euthanasia, and therapeutic abortion? Not all non-Catholics do, of course, favor all of these things. Aside from grave questions of theology or morals, Catholics see in the espousal of these practices a breaking-down of fundamental beliefs that once formed the very basis of our Judaeo-Christian heritage. Whatever disagreements might have existed, and there were many, it was felt that there was a common agreement on what Catholics have called the principles of natural law. They have seen themselves deserted by practically all their allies on the controversy over birth control. To read the criticisms of the Catholic opposition put out by non-Catholics, one would think that opposition to artificial contraception had always been a mark of the rigidity of Catholic belief alone. Catholics fail to understand why, for instance, if about forty years ago artificial contraception was morally wrong for Episcopalians, it is now by their declaration not only morally right but its use even imperative under certain circumstances.

Catholics are then justified in asking: "Where do we go from here?" With something of a shudder they hear praise poured upon the Japanese for reduction of the birth rate and very often with little reference to how this was effected. Since legalized abortion accounted for most of it, Catholics fear that approval of this method may be the approved next step as it is in non-Catholic Sweden. In other words, what are the limits to interference with the birth process? Or does stern necessity know no law whatsoever?

A recent editorial in *Worldview* puts the Catholic viewpoint thus:

Protestants might remind themselves that: (a) the Catholic position on artificial birth control was until recent decades the almost universally accepted position of the Christian Churches; (b) this position rests upon a coherent and rational theory of natural law, and in their recent statement the American bishops were affirming this position; (c) in their statement the bishops were further affirming the rights of American Catholics to act in the public order according to the dictates of their conscience and to reject as public policy that which they consider to be intrinsically immoral; (d) in this, the bishops were making no attempt to "impose" their views on anyone, but were, on the contrary, vindicating a basic principle of democratic procedure within a pluralist society: the principle of each group's right to speak publicly in the light of its own moral convictions.[1]

One hears non-Catholics deplore the number of illegitimate births among migrants from the south who settle in our large cities. These illegitimate children crowd the relief rolls. Immediately the suggestion comes that we should warn every applicant for relief who mothers an illegitimate child that after three offenses she must consent to sterilization. True as it may be that not all non-Catholics would agree to this step, it appears to many of them as a quick and easy solution to an immediate problem.

Catholics also would like to know if the offering of information on artificial contraception will be followed by laws enforcing the practice of it. In the Indian Parliament a short time ago a measure was introduced providing for a tax on each child conceived beyond three. The measure failed of passage, but the question remains, what follows if people will not use contraception devices? All those people who find a remedy for all contingencies in a law incorporated on the statute books will raise a cry in the name of humanity for proscriptive legislation.

Catholics look with dismay upon the increase in divorces with all the attendant evils that follow—unhappiness, broken homes, and juvenile delinquency. The not uncommon practice of one man having three or more living wives or one woman having as many husbands has made a mockery of the bonds of marriage. Most non-Catholics, of course, do not look with favor on this situation, but Catholics feel that it should cause good people outside the Catholic Church to be less sharply critical of the Catholic position. Prohibition of divorce or rigid divorce laws may cause infidelity, but have we not encouraged infidelity with our present system (for the sake of securing a divorce) and have we not cloaked it in the garb of respectability by legalizing it?

To many non-Catholics the Catholic makes of himself a nuisance in setting himself up against artificial contraception, sterilization, or divorce, and he is asked why he tries to impose his standards on all others. The answer is that he believes practices of this kind affect not only Catholics, but tend to destroy

[1] January, 1960, Vol. 3. No. 1.

the fabric of society itself. While the Catholic should always try in his position to use the force of reason, he should not be accused of being unfaithful to the country in which he lives if in accordance with his views he is trying to save it from the tragic consequences of the errors of the majority. Protestants have always boasted of their respect for the convictions of others, and yet they would force Catholics to contribute through taxes to the spread of what is definitely evil from the Catholic point of view. Such is the case in the demand in non-Catholic circles for the use of foreign-aid funds to spread artificial-birth-control education through the masses of people in India and elsewhere. While it is true that taxes have no direct relation to benefit and that every taxpayer cannot be expected to approve of the way in which his taxes are spent, yet when a sizable minority of some thirty-five million people object in conscience to a specific public expenditure, it becomes a matter of fairness and justice and ordinary good will to find other means of accomplishing the end sought.

The Catholic cannot help being disturbed by the growth of a philosophy of relativism which he sees in the non-Catholic world. He sees it in attitudes of mature students in colleges and universities and he sees it in more pronounced fashion in the faculties of these schools. We suffer in this country from a cultural lag, from a nineteenth-century view that science and the methods of empirical science should govern all of life. After two terrible wars a great part of Europe recovered from this attitude. But as accepted here, it means to those holding it that there are no absolute values, that all things are relative, that all statements are matters of opinion, and that there is no such thing as universal and unchanging truth. There are only mores and no morals. This viewpoint is in part due to the commendable desire to view all conclusions and all knowledge objectively. The closed mind is rightly feared. Yet what can be said of the open mind that refuses to close in on a clearly demonstrated truth? The trouble with this kind of mind was aptly described by a former president of Harvard when he said it was open at top and bottom. One enthusiastic student relativist once blandly told me that in "his opinion" it was wrong for Hitler to exterminate Jews but that one could not make a universal statement about it and that perhaps society two hundred years hence would have a different view of the morality of it. One biologist said it was a perfectly legitimate experiment to hold people under water to see how soon they would die because science and morality had nothing to do with one another. As it was put, "When you go into your laboratory, you close the door of your oratory."

The absolute indifference of so many students and so many of the academic personnel of non-Catholic background to all religion should be a matter of deep concern to everyone. Religion according to these people comes under the classification of nonreasoned, emotional experience which one puts aside with adulthood or with the accumulation of knowledge. It is understandable how many of these people fall victim to anti-Catholicism. Catholicism's emphasis on the supernatural, its refusal to regard the moral code as something that can be changed by majority vote places the Catholic Church in the position of the enemy of progress and enlightenment. Erroneously they believe that the dogmas of the Church cover all activities of life and thought. To them a cleric breathes down the neck of every Catholic scholar. To their agnosticism of the adult years they add anti-Catholic views that they have absorbed in childhood, views which they do not submit to the scientific scrutiny that they employ in their own disciplines. If they are liberals, the Catholic Church represents reaction, fascism, or dogmatic intolerance. They renounce anti-Semitism vehemently; they deplore all evidence of antiracism, but to be anti-Catholic, sometimes militantly and unreasonably so, such an attitude has become almost a necessary pose for the cult. The fact that so many Catholics are liberals in the American sense of the term is to them one of those mysteries which can only be explained by the fact that men are inconsistent.

To the outsider the Catholic Church is a difficult and complex institution to understand. If he looks at its natural and mundane manifestations alone, his point of view is as distorted as the man who looks only at the reverse side of a tapestry. While it is true of any institution that one does not truly know it unless he is in it, it is especially true of the Catholic Church. And as it is true of most institutions, there are many within it who do not really know it. Unfortunately, the opinions of outsiders may come from these half-in and half-out members. While one may fill volumes with what many educated people do not know about any religion, their lack of knowledge of Catholicism is often not only profound but even ridiculous. I have been asked by educated non-Catholics what donations one gives at confessions, what statistical use the priest makes of the information gained in confession, if he does not make any statistical use what good is the institution of confession, if in collections at the door of the church (a practice which most Catholics do not like) one gives according to his estimate of the gravity of his sins, if Catholics may read the Bible, if Catholics abstain from meat on Fridays in the belief that there is something intrinsically evil in flesh meat, and many like questions. The ignorance of the educated may astound a Catholic, but he should remember that the Catholic lines of communication to the secular centers of education have been until recent years almost neglected. Yet the Catholic shudders at the thought of the hazy and mistaken ideas of the Church held by the educated. He may well be terrified at the notions held by the uneducated and half-educated.

From a Protestant source comes the story of a Protestant minister who began his Sunday sermon as follows: "'Thou shalt love the Lord thy God with thy whole heart and soul, and thy neighbor as thyself.' Now putting aside the first part of the commandment and considering the second . . ." These two parts of the commandment, love of God and love of neighbor, we are taught, are closely joined and one cannot hate his neighbor and still love God, but the statement of the good minister illustrates an approach far too common. The desire to get on to the things of this world to the neglect of the things of the other world characterizes the thought and practice of too many Protestant leaders. Catholics would have Protestants more holy and not less, but a form of secularism has overtaken some Protestant churches and Jewish synagogues. The teachings of the gospel or the Scriptures should, of course, be related to everyday life and Catholic sermons are apt to neglect this aspect of religious teaching, but the Church is no place for the teaching of social science. A Protestant minister friend of mine once told me with some pride that his parishioners go to church Sunday after Sunday and do not hear the name of God mentioned. Curious about what was substituted for the teachings of God, I ventured to ask what was done at the services and he replied that every Sunday a new work of fiction was reviewed. I do not by any means wish to convey the idea that this is in any way typical, nor am I unaware of the deeply spiritual movements that are evident in Protestant circles. One would be blind indeed if he did not pay tribute to the religious, devoted, and self-sacrificing lives that very many non-Catholic people live. We are all their debtors. The secularism that has infected some non-Catholic groups renders them easy prey to every whim of fashion, every emotional mass hysteria, and every easy but dangerous solution to mankind's ills. For people so affected religion becomes not a matter of faith and reason, but a matter of pure emotion. Religion comes to depend upon internal waves of emotion or peculiar visceral feelings of joy or sorrow. Charity is not done in God's name but because it makes one feel so good inside to have shown benevolence to the unfortunate. Or religion itself is pictured as providing a joy-ride through life with success in business assured and all the sorrows, sacrifices, struggles, and pain eliminated. Many non-Catholics deplore these things and Catholics join them in praying that such manifestation of pseudo religion may be confined within ever-narrowing bounds.

The phrase "our pluralistic society" occurs in every interfaith writing or discussion. No one can deny that we live in such a society. No one can deny that certain special adaptations are needed in such a society. Few societies today are not pluralistic. Pluralism is not always a blessing. The pluralism existing in this country on the slavery issue before the Civil war might have destroyed the Union. Pluralism might be so divisive in its nature that a social order would be possible. There must always exist some bond of union, some agreement on common concerns to cement a society. There existed at one time theories of individualism so extreme that anarchy alone could have been the result if the theories were ever realized.

As long ago as Aristotle's time the value in diversity was realized. If all men contributed, each of his special ability, the political order would be enriched, but one common end, one common good had to be the aim. Even with the recognition of one common faith, the Middle Ages showed much diversity in art, literature, architecture, and philosophy. The exciting life at the University of Paris in the thirteenth century gives evidence enough that in the field of philosophy and theology many different schools of thought existed. Yet certain fundamental, common principles held society together. Whether our present-day society is better off with the extremes of philosophic and religious thought is open to question. Certainly there could still be diversity with more common agreement as to religious aims. Ecumenism testifies that less variety in religious thought would be both acceptable and beneficial. No society can last without the acceptance of certain basic moral beliefs, the relativistic view that no value is fixed to the contrary notwithstanding.

Catholics do not approve of uniformity; even in their own Church the variety of ways to heaven, the sharp disputes among theologians, the disagreements among social scientists and philosophers, and the differences on political questions all indicate that even if uniformity were desired it does not exist. One Catholic ecclesiast compared the approach of various orders within the Church to certain divisions in Protestantism. He said the Benedictines were like the Episcopalians, the Franciscans like the Methodists, and the Dominicans like the Presbyterians. He left the Jesuits unclassified.

Catholics nevertheless are puzzled by certain non-Catholic attitudes toward them. Certain of their critics among those who value pluralism highly protest that Catholics do not fit in, that they are different. One critic is upset because nuns have a special garb (Catholics themselves would like to change some of them), that Catholic services are not like Protestant services, and that the priests wear strange garments during services, or that not all Catholics will go to public schools. This is strange opinion coming from a pluralist or from Americans, who prize the richness in the variety of customs existing in this country. Lurking in this kind of criticism is a dangerous desire to impose a kind of *gleichschaltung* on America in which all would fall down in adoration at the shrine of a political philosophy-totalitarian democracy.

Catholic respect for diversity goes too far for non-Catholics. They do not approve of the Church's willingness to live with all kinds of regimes throughout the world—democratic or absolute. Some non-Catholics would like the Church to condemn outright all regimes that fall short of the democratic ideal. Spain is their special target because non-Catholics in that country are denied full rights of citizens. What has been said before needs repeating, that most Catholics throughout the world do not approve of the Spanish treatment of political and religious dissenters. They are willing to leave this situation, however, to the forces of the modern world which will compel changes, and they pray that change will not be accompanied by revolution and bloodshed.

When reference is made to Spain and to people living under a Spanish or Latin tradition, Catholics have a complaint to register. Protestants enter these lands not infrequently and become embroiled in political movements and become centers of disaffection which bring upon them the condemnation of the ruling powers. This is not to say that these Protestant groups might not represent the ideal of justice, but as minority religious groups—and often as recent comers—prudence would seem to indicate a more cautious attitude. The cleric, whether Catholic or non-Catholic, is poorly prepared for engagements of a political nature. Without boasting, it may be said that small minority Catholic groups in overwhelmingly Protestant lands, even when full rights are denied them, behave better than their Protestant brethren in similar circumstances. Long-established, traditional forms of Protestantism do not as a rule create trouble in Latin countries, but newly-formed, crusading evangelistic sects, particularly from our South, forget the common rules of good behavior when they enter Latin lands. Their behavior is often boorish and insulting, and like Communists they hope for suppression and persecution. No group can enter lands Catholic by tradition and offer public insult to Catholic belief and practice without stirring up trouble if not public disorder. The memory of recent occurrences of this kind has created hostility on the part of public and Church officials alike.

The alliance which Protestant groups make with outright enemies of the Catholic Church, notably Masonry, in Latin countries contributes in great measure to the hostility of Catholics toward Protestants. Unlike Masonry in this country, Latin

Masonry has all the features of a crusading agonosticism or atheism. Its members have no firm religious convictions. It is not interested in the conversion of any soul to the Gospel of Jesus Christ but seeks the spread of its own antireligious doctrines. It will use Protestantism against the dominant Catholic religion and will shower favors and money upon North American evangelists. Latin Masonry is deeply involved in politics and it inevitably involves its allies in its political practices. Whatever temporary gains Protestant groups may enjoy from such an alliance must be paid for in an ever-growing religious agnosticism among the Latin people.

There are pagans in the jungles of South America. There are also people who practice a borderline Catholicism not readily comprehended by other Catholics throughout the world. The latter, however, consider themselves Catholic. The great mass of people are Catholic by tradition and nonpracticing; some by tradition and conviction are active members of the Church. Catholics cannot but feel the insult implied when Protestants say they are sending missionaries to South America to "Christianize" the people. Not so many years ago I attended a lecture at a New York City Y.M.C.A. given by a Protestant missionary to Cuba. The lecture was illustrated. We were shown some rather poorly dressed Cubans emerging from a Catholic church on Sunday, then praying at a shrine, and finally, presumably that same afternoon, having a very merry time at a country fair. We were told that the Catholic Church was "to blame" for this evident frivolity on the Sabbath. We were then shown these same people after they had been "Christianized." They emerged from a Protestant chapel all cleaned and dressed up, went home and ate at a well-laden board, and then all went for a rather solemn walk. They were indeed better groomed, but it did appear as though their new concept of God made them very gloomy. When Protestant missionaries go to South America, would it not be more charitable toward Catholic Christians to say that their purpose is to convert the natives to another form of Christianity?

Despite all the talk of religious freedom in our land, Jews and Catholics know that Protestant prejudice sometimes prevents their securing positions or advancement. This is especially true in rural areas. This complaint, however, cannot be lodged against all Protestants. As far as Catholics are concerned, the remedy for this unfortunate situation lies partly in more frequent association with Protestants, but this is only one remedy. The burden of eradicating prejudice of this kind rests with Protestant leaders. If local Protestant churches insist upon inviting itinerant lecturers to talk on the recurring topic which generally runs: "I love individual Catholics but I hate the Roman hierarchy," neither truth nor good will can be served. Existing prejudices among many Protestant groups may be traced to such prophets of misunderstanding and discord.

Consideration has already been given to the question of a Catholic candidate for the Presidency. Catholics resent profoundly the implications that a person of their faith could not serve the country loyally. It implies that every Catholic citizen is not a good citizen. Opposition to a Catholic's holding the Presidency ranges all the way from a sweeping rejection of Catholics on all counts to more specific objection on certain counts.[2] People in the latter class want to know the Catholic candidate's position on American representation at the Vatican, governmental aid to public schools, birth-control legislation, and the Catholic position on church and state. Is it fair for objectors to question a Catholic candidate? Some Catholics and some non-Catholics object to such questioning on the ground that it is an unnecessary insinuation of religion into politics. Yet people have a right to know any candidate's stand on matters that might require legislation or executive action. A great deal depends upon who asks the question and the motives that prompt it. If the questioner happens to be a person long known for his opposition to all things Catholic and whose opposition has been notoriously unreasonable, it would surely be the right of a candidate to refuse to reply. Other questioners, however, may have a laudable curiosity, and no candidate should object to making a reply to such people. A certain irritation may be excused in Catholic candidates who are confronted again and again by the same questions, the same objections, even after the fullest publicity has been given to their positions.

---

[2] Some non-Catholics do not realize how much the attack they make against Catholics resembles the hysterical drive of a few years ago against subversives. Hysteria and a disregard of civil rights characterize both.

The difficulty lies in keeping the religious issue in any campaign within reasonable bounds once it is introduced. No issue is more explosive, as any politician knows. It readily becomes what politicians call a gum-shoe issue, that is, it deteriorates and develops into a whispering campaign. In its most vicious form it crops up in the last days of a campaign when there is little chance to counteract it. It would seem that responsible Protestants have a special obligation, if we are ever confronted with a Catholic candidate for the Presidency, in forcefully condemning the pressing of the religious issue beyond all the rules of reason. It would be most salutary if, at the very beginning of such a campaign, a sizable number of nationally respected Protestants would issue a statement calculated to keep the issues of the contest on the political plain.

Whatever the complaints of Catholics against the non-Catholic world, they have a special obligation to meet the criticisms of reasonable people, not with the cry of bigotry or with a personal attack, but with a frank and intelligent response. Catholics as well as non-Catholics will always have a lunatic fringe among their numbers to whom the exercise of caution and the application of common sense mean nothing at all. Among both groups there will always be those, clergy and laymen alike, who make public statements without thought of the consequences. In the field of interfaith discussion even people of discretion and prudence are easily led astray by the fighting crusaders. After the lesson of centuries both Catholics and non-Catholics should know by now that religious strife has bred a large population of agnostics, and it will continue to do so unless religious leaders learn how to disagree in a spirit of charity.

CHAPTER VII

Reflections, Suggestions, and Queries

Much of the material of the preceding chapters has dealt with interfaith relations which may seem to have only a very remote relation with the theory and practice of church and state. It should be remembered, however, that a greater part of non-Catholic opposition to Catholics in this country stems in large part from Catholic ideas on church and state. When this question arises most of the other questions inevitably follow. As a Catholic layman reflects on what Dr. Robert McAfee Brown calls "the battle-scarred arena of 'Catholic-Protestant relations,'"[1] he feels that he must set forth clearly some developments within his church which non-Catholics may not fully appreciate and certain matters which Catholics should consider with all due seriousness.

First, I believe that non-Catholics should realize the new position of the layman in the Catholic church. Protestants, it must be recognized, had a point in saying that within the parent Church the laymen had fallen to a position of insignificance. His position as a witness to the gospel was almost forgotten and his position as a participant in divine services had all but disappeared. Many non-Catholic scholars are now fully aware of the importance and significance of the liturgical movement and they realize the important part now played by the laity as a consequence. Non-Catholic scholars are also aware of the efforts on the part of Catholic scholars to produce a satisfactory theology of the layman. While perhaps having a different connotation than the Protestant phrase, the priesthood of the laity is a phrase heard constantly in Catholic circles and its significance is emphasized.

[1] *Commonweal,* February 19, 1960.

With the past two generations, or ever since the pontificate of Pius X, the growth of various lay movements has spread throughout the Catholic world. *Catholic Action,* secular institutes, lay missionary groups, and numberless lay organizations with the enthusiastic support of the popes and bishops have come to play an active role in the formation and direction of Catholic life. The late Samuel Cardinal Stritch of Chicago never tired of repeating that this was the day of the layman. In our day one finds groups of laymen who daily recite the Breviary—once an occupation solely for priests; one finds numerous classes in theology for laymen and the development of lay teachers in the field. It is questionable if one could catalogue exactly all the organizations of laymen, many of them for the purpose of promoting the spiritual life of their members, others for the purpose of furthering adult education in varied fields, and others for the purpose of informing social life with Christian principles in labor, race relations, urban development, and the like. Furthermore devotion to the spiritual life is attested by the greater number of men and women who at considerable sacrifice make the Mass and reception of Holy Communion a daily practice. In few countries in the world can it be said that the Catholic Church shows greater spiritual energy than in America.

The combination of religious zeal and intelligent understanding of his faith characterizes in ever-increasing degree the laymen today, especially in the United States. While many Catholic groups, outside of their spiritual interest, never reach higher intellectual plateaus than the fortunes of the major-league baseball teams, an interest characteristic of Sunday-morning Communion breakfasts of the Holy Name Society, other groups reach high levels of intellectual concern. The Catholic does not blindly follow the leadership of the clergy. Priests themselves will sometimes complain about the "Yes, Father," attitude of some laymen who adhere to an older and vanishing tradition. In the Catholic atmosphere of today the Catholic laymen, while always showing respect for the clergy, wants to know and wants the reasons clearly laid down. This tendency grows alongside a very greatly deepened religious faith.

American Catholics still tend to stand in awe of their bishops.

The monsignor who congratulated a fellow monsignor on the latter's being raised to the episcopacy with the commiserating words: "You will never hear the truth spoken of yourself or your actions again," was describing a situation that not infrequently exists. There are bishops who by their less reserved attitudes invite frank statements from their priests and laity, but here, too, the open invitation may not be taken up. No responsible person wishes to see develop in this country a kind of nagging, complaining attitude toward the bishops or a kind of hail-fellow-well-met attitude on the part of the bishops themselves which would lower the dignity of the office. I do not want to imply that there is not criticism of bishops by the laymen, that is, outside of the bishops' hearing and presence. Yet the greatest check to anticlericalism, an affliction that does not exist in any degree in America, would seem to be an open and frank relationship between the laymen and the clergy of all ranks.

It cannot be said, however, that there is not a healthy self-criticism among Catholics. Scarcely a symposium is held or a lecture given by a Catholic that some phase of Catholic life is not criticized. A few years ago Monsignor John Tracy Ellis initiated a most fruitful controversy on the absence of intellectuals within the Church. Subjects such as education, art, architecture, music, philosophy, theology, social attitudes can start an argument in any sizable Catholic group. It should never be thought that because Catholics accept common dogmas of faith, they live in the quiet of a tomb. Agreement on fundamentals often makes the argument more spirited.

Among Catholic laymen the ghetto spirit, is far less in evidence today. It has been pointed out that an election campaign in which the Catholic issue played a large part could conceivably re-create the old ghetto spirit. Catholic laymen, however, work as business and professional men, or tradesmen, or craftsmen among their non-Catholic colleagues. No one turns down a good, honest business deal for religious causes. For at least eight hours of every day the Catholic layman must live with a good cross-section of American society. Obviously this is not true of the Catholic clergy. And herein lies a basic cause of the misunderstanding that exists in American life between Catholics and non-Catholics. Until the non-Catholic, particularly the non-Catholic clergyman, knows the Catholic priest as priest, scholar, or citizen the unfortunate attitude maintained by many outside of the Church will remain.

Some priests and bishops maintain friendly relations with non-Catholic clergymen and laymen, but sad to relate this is not the rule. To multitudes of non-Catholics the priesthood remains a mysterious force operating in mysterious ways behind all of Catholic life. What is mysterious and unknown may very likely be feared and suspected. The ordinary priest educated in a parochial school, then in a minor seminary, and finally in a major seminary lives despite all outside influences in a world entirely Catholic. But this is not the American world in reality. As a parish priest or pastor his vocational life gives him contacts almost entirely Catholic and his social life is confined to fellowship with other priests, particularly of his own class in the seminary. In this situation he sees all things through Catholic eyes. Association with non-Catholic clergymen is rare. It is true that in some small towns the relationship between the Catholic pastor and the non-Catholic pastor may be cordial and co-operative, but this is seldom the case in the larger city where the Catholic population may be numerous.

When the priest rises in the hierarchy, the separation of the bishop from the non-Catholic world except on official occasions is apt to be continued. Strangely enough this situation has grown with the years and the increase of the Catholic population. It was not the situation in the day of a Cardinal Gibbons or an Archbishop Ireland. Two basic causes may be assigned for the existence of the separationist attitude—one, the way of living that the priest has become accustomed to, the other, a fear of indifferentism which many of the priests and bishops believe will arise among the lay people. It is feared that frequent association will give rise to a feeling that one religion is as good as another and that it makes no difference what or how a man believes. This need not follow, but unfortunately some non-Catholics are apt to take this line when association becomes frequent. When a priest or a minister appear on the same platform and the minister gives voice in public to this sentimental and clubby emotion, then the priest believes all his worst fears are confirmed. If the genius of American life is the ability of people of differing opinions, attitudes, and vocations to live in peace, then this attempt to reduce differences to a common unrecognizable mass runs counter to the best of our traditions. An exaggerated fear of this outlook has led to official Catholic condemnation of all forms of association with non-Catholic groups, particularly a prohibition of participation on the part of the clergy.

Out of this aloofness on the part of the Catholic clergy arises their inability to communicate with non-Catholics in terms which the latter understand. In addition there is formed an unreal picture of the non-Catholic world. When clergy so uninformed make public statements for their own flocks or for more general consumption, their words are often open to the most extreme misinterpretation. Statements, too, that may have meaning for Catholics do not move the non-Catholic world, and if moved, that world may be incensed at the tone of the message. How much ill will has resulted from the Catholic clergy's lack of knowledge of the non-Catholic world it is impossible to say, but the Catholic who moves in that world no doubt feels it is not inconsiderable.

Catholic laymen mix daily in our pluralistic society. They bear the brunt of charges against the Church and with great frequency must answer the honest inquiries regarding it. The laymen will often see ways and means of combating ignorance of the Church or animosity to it. The clergy, because of their isolation from the non-Catholic world, have in not a few cases failed to co-operate with the laymen in practical means of fostering better understanding. Situations most embarrassing to the devoted layman and creating further misunderstanding among non-Catholics are caused by sudden orders to cease and desist from further action. Such caution would seem to contradict that apostolic spirit so characteristic of the early Church. Non-Catholics rightly complain when they charge that failure of co-operation is not lacking in areas where Catholics form a distinct minority, but where Catholics predominate the barriers are well-nigh insuperable. Even where the lines of communication remain open for the laymen, they are most unfortunately closed to the priest. Catholics it is true, whether priest or layman, may not participate in the purely religious exercises of non-Catholics, but there are wide areas of possible co-operation beyond this line and no Church law prevents ordinary social intercourse.

While the school issue is such a burning issue in the controversy between Catholics and non-Catholics, it would be well if Catholics would take a good over-all look at their school system. For the most part it operates under a decentralized control; only one national Catholic institution exists, the Catholic University of America in Washington. The other educational institutions from the primary school through the university are under the jurisdiction of a particular diocese or under the jurisdiction of the various provinces into which the religious orders are divided. There is not one Catholic school system in the United States, but about four hundred. We are not likely to see a unified Catholic school system in this country even though certain administrative and financial advantages might result. Yet it is well at a time when Catholics are feeling the financial burden of the system, a burden which is likely to grow heavier, that they use every means available to reduce costs without undermining the educational standards. It has been pointed out that within a few years over fifty per cent of the teachers in all levels of the Catholic schools will be recruited from the laity. Obviously salary scales for lay teachers will have to be on a par with those paid in other private institutions and close to the scale of salaries paid in the public institutions. With adequate salary scales there will have to be the usual fringe benefits—retirement pensions, group insurance, and some form of insurance against sickness. These increased costs the Catholics will have to face along with the ever-increasing cost of plant and equipment. Even if some form of public aid is available, it will never lighten the burden of the cost of education appreciably. For instance, people who believe that federal or state scholarship grants will aid the schools, should remember that tuition costs now cover scarcely half of what it costs to educate a person.

Furthermore, if Catholics hope to convince the non-Catholic world that they deserve public support, the standards must not only equal, but surpass the public institution. The Catholic institutions should fulfill that role which independent schools are expected to fill, namely, become laboratories of experiment in new advances in education. Simply to be duplicates of the public schools does not justify the independent system.

It has been suggested by some Catholics that the lower grades of the primary-school system be dropped and Catholic children sent to the public schools at this time. It has been suggested also that more centralization of financing of the primary and high-school grades be adopted in each diocese with considerable saving in cost of equipment and greater efficiency in administration. It has also been suggested that an arrangement be made with public-school authorities for students from the Catholic high schools to take their courses in science at the public high schools if the latter schools are close by. Laboratory equipment being a great expense, this undoubtedly would result in a saving. All these suggestions, if adopted, would help in an economic sense.

On the higher levels of education we have gone on the theory that since there are large numbers of Catholic students who could not be accommodated in existing colleges, we should increase the number of colleges to meet the need. The ambition is laudable but the attempts to fulfill it have meant the spawning of numbers of Catholic colleges that are unable to support themselves properly and consequently are unable to meet high standards of education. The multiplication of colleges is not the answer to educational needs. Two terms should be noted in the phrase Catholic education—*Catholic* and *education*. Too many Catholic parents believe that if the first term *Catholic* is taken care of, either the second term naturally follows or it does not matter. The tendency to look upon the school as a kind of reform institution to make religiously indifferent people devout may have something to be said for it, but a college or university has as its main object education in the intellectual virtues. As a matter of fact, if as an educational institution it fails, it is apt to fail in turning out devoted Catholics.

Granting that there are many high-grade Catholic colleges and universities, it is disturbing to note that there are many inferior ones. And the administration of Catholic colleges suffers from an affliction similar to that which afflicts secular colleges. Every college is supposed to grow into a university. The addition of a school of business, generally a successful financial enterprise, suffices to stir the ambitions for university status. It is highly questionable whether schools of business or schools of journalism or the like belong in a university, but they seem to be sufficient as additions to bring the high-sounding title of university. There are a few excellent, well-established Catholic universities, but the larger number of them could do a much better job as first-class liberal-arts colleges. It would cost less to operate them and they would be less of a drain upon limited Catholic resources, which should be expended upon a few outstanding universities. One graduate department or one or two vocational schools do not make a university. The heart of university work, research, requires extensive and costly library and laboratory equipment. How many of our universities possess or have any hopes of possessing such facilities? About 250 institutions in this land call themselves universities. The United States Office of Education recognizes 141 as such; the American Association of Universities recognizes only 39.

The question might even be raised at this point whether or not Catholic universities—those *worthy* of the name—should not consider concentration in certain fields which can more readily be supported. The cost of maintaining adequate facilities in the biological and physical sciences especially weighs heavily on even the most well-endowed of the private secular universities. To meet the competition of private industry men in these fields must be compensated with salaries far exceeding any other salaries paid in academic life. The laboratory equipment which these specialists require runs into millions of dollars for one institution if the resulting research is to meet most modern needs. Perhaps Catholics have reached the point where graduate work and its facilities need to be thoroughly examined with an eye to determining not only what can be done, but what can be done well. It may possibly be found that Catholic institutions can do their best work along graduate lines in the humanities and the social sciences. Other fields might be left to the state universities or the well-endowed private secular schools. If a student who has reached graduate years is unable to hold fast to his faith at a secular institution, it is questionable whether further training at a Catholic university can make him any stronger.

One of the foremost reasons cited for the existence of an independent school system alongside the state schools is the opportunity for experimentation. The Catholic schools are in a position where deviations from the traditional could be tried with profit. St. Xavier's College for Women in Chicago is one of the most notable examples of a departure from the norm with an integrated program of study revolving around philosophy and theology. This plan of education has received merited recognition from non-Catholic sources. The fear exists in most Catholic colleges that experimentation may lead to difficulties with accrediting agencies; they therefore repeat all the traditional forms of education along with the traditional mistakes.

Since we are here considering the type of educational system which can best make use of available resources without dependence upon the state, one is led to inquire why Catholics have not considered more seriously the so-called six-four-four plan which has been discussed by educators for several years. This plan substitutes for the present system six years of grade school followed by four years of high school, and concludes with four years of college. This would mean the squeezing of a great deal of water out of the present system, would eliminate the prolongation of adolescence so characteristic of American education, and would give greater intensification to the study of worth-while subjects. It is true there would be difficulty with some accrediting agencies; and high-school administrators throughout the land might organize a boycott to protect a vested interest. The foundations might have to come to the support of the first diocese that put the plan into effect. Yet this is the foresight and imagination which Catholic education can bring to our whole American system of education. Catholics must seize the initiative in educational reform if they are to gain prestige and proper recognition in our pluralistic American society. Some religious order would gain fame and the praise of future generations if it would set forth to accomplish the educational reform herein indicated.

Among lesser reforms possible at this time would be the elimination of the last two years of many of our four year colleges. A first-class system of junior colleges would enhance the prestige of Catholic education. These institutions, more readily maintained than the four-year college, might excel in the liberal arts which so definitely belong to the Catholic tradition and which have been so significantly neglected in Catholic education. The founding of future Catholic colleges on or near the campuses of great state or secular schools must also be considered, not for accomplishment in the next century but in the immediate future. It is within the realm of the possible to work out plans for credit for courses taken at both the Catholic college and at the larger institutions. Besides the material savings involved in this plan, the Catholic colleges would gain all the educational advantages which the larger state or private secular schools could offer, particularly in the field of the sciences. It would also eliminate that spirit of exclusiveness which is apt to infuse the school that is set apart.

An excellent article in *America* raises some of the questions which have here been pointed out when it says: "Will they [our colleges] condemn themselves to a decade of mediocrity because of undertrained and underpaid faculty, inadequate laboratory and research facilities, poverty of library buildings and dearth of scholarship funds? Such questions deserve the attention of all of us in view of the modern insistence that running a college is no longer like operating a grocery store." The article points out that we can learn something from the Canadian experience: "The most recent example is in Upper Ontario. There plans have been agreed to among Anglican, Catholic, and United Church of Canada education leaders for the establishment of the 'Laurentian University of Sudbury': A Government-backed bill to charter the new institution is to be presented at the current session of the Provincial Legislature. Ontario's Premier Leslie Frost has indicated that the University will be eligible for Government aid because . . . the university as a whole will be non-denominational. Last year the Ontario Legislature incorporated St. Jerome's College (Catholic) and Waterloo Lutheran University as the 'University of Waterloo' and other instances of this united approach could be multiplied."[2]

For many years Catholics have had little or no communication with the centers of learning and research in the secular world. This has had the result of shutting Catholics off from the important intellectual pursuits of American society. Secular schools have developed standards of teaching and research that

[2] February 20, 1960.

have been of the utmost importance in the development of intellectual life. The absence of any Catholic influence, until recent years, in the secular schools has had unfortunate results both for Catholics and for the schools. However, priests, religious and Catholic laymen appear in greater number for graduate work at the great secular universities and contact appears to be growing between Catholic and secular schools. Catholic laymen in greater numbers occupy positions on the faculties of these schools. A more recent development of priests appearing on the faculties of secular schools, mostly on part-time arrangements, has much to commend it. Yale, Stanford, Dartmouth, and the University of Chicago have had or now have priests teaching with faculty status. And the appointment of the eminent Catholic scholar, Christopher Dawson, to the faculty of the Harvard Divinity School, may constitute a precedent of far-reaching consequences. The employment of a priest at a secular university is a singular recognition of his scholarship and it is to be prayerfully hoped that ordinaries and religious superiors will have a full appreciation of this and welcome and encourage it.

Dr. Robert McAfee Brown raises the question whether or not the Catholics in America are as creative and even venturesome in their writings as the Catholics of Europe. He does not think they are. In Catholic circles his belief finds support. A timidity among American Catholics in putting forth new propositions or espousing new practices in the religious sphere does characterize the Church in the United States. Perhaps this is due to the absence until recent years of a vital intellectual life. We depended upon European leadership. Outside of the Church, however, the orthodoxy of the American Catholic is frequently noted. In the atmosphere that now exists one would not expect a St. Thomas Aquinas to arise challenging an old tradition and synthesizing the work of a pagan philosopher with Christian thought. This was a daring thing to do in the thirteenth century and it is this daring that one misses among American Catholics. Catholic students of moral theology will quote many of the new ideas brought forth in the field by French or German scholars, but there is always safety in quoting someone else. Rome is regarded not as a helpful guide to correct doctrine or practice, but as a seat of judgment pronouncing doom upon the erring.

While a papal instruction from Rome will everywhere be treated respectfully as a general principle, in the United States it will receive a strictness of interpretation that must surprise authorities in Rome themselves. A few years ago Pope Pius XII issued a timely instruction on conversations between Catholics and non-Catholics. It gave the bishops of the world jurisdiction in the matter of Catholic participation. To prevent a kind of an irresponsible public free-for-all in a matter so important the pope urged caution and laid down the requirement that in theological discussions well-qualified theologians represent the Catholic point of view. There were negative and positive sides to this instruction, but in the United States the trend was to take a negative view and to discourage all discussion.

The manner of interpreting provisions of the canon law characteristic of some diocesan chancellors in this country gives rise to the question of whether or not an unnecessary rigor accompanies the application of Church regulations. An American priest, the Reverend Claiborne Lafferty, who teaches comparative law at the Pontifical Lateran University in Rome, warns: "When a man raised in the tradition of Anglo-American law has to apply canon law, he can get into trouble." Commenting on this statement, *America* says: "For one thing, according to this lawyer-canonist, canon law is framed as an expression of general principles and allows of exceptions. The precedent-based common law, on the other hand, is framed to include all cases and admits of no exceptions. This difference of approach . . . can induce serious misinterpretations of the mind of the Church."[3]

In this connection, the application of rules affecting the Index of Forbidden Books comes at once to mind. The orders of some chancery offices on this particular matter sometimes approach the ludicrous. John Cogley, writing in the *Commonweal*, has this to say regarding the Index: "And again, if the truth be told, most American Catholics have little affection for the Index of Forbidden Books. In a day when mass communications carry every conceivable idea far and wide, the belief that the Index can protect the faithful from being exposed to heretical and erroneous ideas strikes many as a howling anachronism. At least in this

[3] February 6, 1960.

country, where illiteracy has been practically abolished, Catholics, like everyone else, can pick such ideas out of the air. They are on all sides. For the most part, the American Catholic who remains faithful to the Church does so because he has heard all the arguments and still chooses to remain in it. . . . For that tradition [the Catholic] is not simply one of restriction and negation, though many think of it in such terms. It is a solid body of thought with a very strong intellectual and human appeal. It can, as it were, stand on its own legs. It does not need the special protection of Indexes or general prohibitions to hold its own among other system of thought."[4]

If I may judge from years of experience living among Catholics, Mr. Cogley does not express an uncommon view. Many American Catholics, without any intention of being unfaithful to their obligations, will tell you that they have never seen the Index and will be guided in their reading by what they do not know. It is questionable whether much is gained by ordering an adult group of eager students of the Great Books to refrain from reading some of the classics found in the list. John Locke's *Second Treatise on Government,* for instance, may constitute an excellent cure for insomnia, but its power of corruption totally escapes the ordinary reader. The kind of offhand, unthinking prohibition is illustrated by the following.

A mature graduate-student priest in the Department of English in one of our major secular universities called the chancery by telephone to ask permission to read a certain book. He had scarcely time to say what the book was before a voice came back: "If against faith, Father, no; if against morals, yes." Ordinarily, scholars and other responsible persons obtain permission to read prohibited books, but the rigidity met with in certain areas makes for wholesale violation of the law or makes of the Index what outside critics claim it is—an unnecessary restriction on man's right to know.

Frankly, it must be stated that the failure of non-Catholics to recognize Catholic scholarship or the Catholic intellectual is in part due to the outsider's understanding of restrictions such as the Index. When such restrictions are applied as the Church

[4] March 4, 1960.

in its wisdom intends them to be applied, there is no reason why Catholic scholarship should not rank with the best in the world. When, however, stupidity, mediocrity, or bureaucracy creates unnecessary stumbling blocks to sincere intellectual endeavors, resentment and disobedience are fostered within the Church and damaging criticism is fostered without.

A permission from Rome for Mass at afternoon and evening hours has met in many a diocese with a very meager acceptance of the permission. A permission to use the English language in certin rites has not been accepted at all in some sections. And while no prohibition whatsoever exists on discussion of the use of the vernacular in the Mass, it will be found an unacceptable subject in some dioceses.

In contrast one finds special permission for a portion of the Mass in the vernacular in France and Germany, and in the latter country the use of the vernacular in many of the beautiful parts of the Holy Week services will be permitted this year. Very frequently what dispensations one asks for in Rome, one gets, but authorities in this country are loath to make the requests. And at this point could not one justly ask whether if certain services or portions of services of the Church were performed in the language of the country, greater appreciation of the Church by those within and those without would result.

A recurring question in both Catholic and non-Catholic circles comes to the fore in this connection. Is American influence in Rome as great as it could and should be? The Church indeed is Catholic and universal; there is not an American Church, an English Church, a German Church, and so on. Doctrine must be the same everywhere, but discipline need not be. The genius of the Church throughout the ages has been its adaptability to conditions of time and place. I doubt whether it is the mind of the Church that the Catholic Church in America be more Roman than Rome.

One of the most serious matters that deserves greater consideration at Rome is what may be called the whole Anglo-Saxon tradition. Scholars have pointed out that one of the great tragedies in the Church was the loss of millions of people at a time of the Reformation who were brought up in that tradition. The Church became Continental European, with a heavy preponderance of the Latin element. Without denying the great values in the Latin tradition, another tradition existed and much of the impact of the latter tradition was lost. The Anglo-Saxon tradition has much more of a direct, unbroken connection with the Catholic Middle Ages in its law and respect for religion than other traditions. Its respect for the individual, for the orderly process of government, for the moderate as opposed to the extreme, and for limited political authority has much more in common with traditional philosophy than other cultures which were infected by the false theories of the Enlightenment. In our own time the Church shows the most evident signs of growth, vitality, and health in those countries which live under the Anglo-Saxon tradition or cultures close to it. This point of view needs to be better known at Rome and the burden of making it better known rests upon the leadership of the Catholic Church in America.

Today we read and hear a great deal about the *dialogue*, a form of rational discussion among leaders of Catholics, Jews, and Protestants on such matters as church and state, pluralism, the school question, religion and the free society, and other important questions about which wide differences of opinion exist.[5] The Fund for the Republic has promoted seminars at which papers on the above and related topics are read, followed by questions and discussions. In these sessions the Jesuits have taken the leading role in stating the Catholic position. The dialogue is an important development in our national life. In large groups, however, where easy give and take in discussion is not possible, the dialogue may become a monologue confined to the chief speaker. The discussion, where discussion is possible, may mushroom forth over a large area without point or direction. The question arises, too, as to whether or not discussion between Catholics and Protestants, and Jews and Christians, would not be more profitable as there are specific problems peculiar to the relationship of these groups which can best be discussed when isolated. One further drawback to the best results obtainable lies in the public nature of the discussions. Where the full glare of

---

[5] See the excellent article by Robert McAfee Brown, "Rules for the Dialogue," published in the *Commonweal*, February 19, 1960, and in the *Christian Century*, February 17, 1960.

the spotlight of publicity shines, the right atmosphere for the calm and judicious probing of differences may be lacking. Nevertheless, whatever the weaknesses of the dialogue as public seminar, large or small, it is a development of great importance to the promotion of better understanding in the religious life of America.

Special conditions, especially in Germany, led to the organization of study groups between Catholics and Protestants for consideration of differences in religious practice and belief. During the period of Nazi control and during the critical period following World War II, Catholics and Protestants found that they confronted common enemies and even found it necessary to use the same church buildings because of the destruction of property as a consequence of the war. The common suffering of priests and ministers, and Catholic and Protestant laymen in concentration camps brought common sympathy and common understanding. The ever-present threat of communism and the forces of unbelief have bolstered the determination for understanding in recent years.

As a result of these conditions, Catholic and Protestant leaders, lay and clerical, have been holding conferences on liturgy, dogma, and Reformation history which have produced deep respect on both sides. Unlike our own dialogue, the purpose of the German groups is not primarily to promote better public relations, although this does eventuate, but to discover the reasons for deep underlying differences. The German seminar is largely a seminar of scholars. Making allowance for the peculiar tragedies which gave birth to these sessions, one can see that they offer a way and a method which could be profitably employed.[6]

A procedure of this kind raises discussion above the emotion-charged level of accusation to the high plain of serious study and discussion by experts and scholars. In addition it is publicity-free. Through it both Lutherans and Catholics have come to see the Reformation in a different light; they have come to see more clearly the problems of faith and doctrine; and finally they have come to see the necessity for unity, however long and

[6] The best recent work by a Protestant on Catholicism is *The Riddle of Roman Catholicism* by Jaroslov Pelikan (New York: Abingdon Press, 1959). Note particularly Part III.

tortuous the road to that desired goal may be. A few years ago the late Cardinal Stritch, Archbishop of Chicago, gave his approval to such a session which would devote itself to discussion of Scriptures. Three Catholic scholars and three Protestant scholars were to participate. The plan never came to fruition because two of the participants were called to parts outside the Chicago area and one participant was lost through death. Catholics might well consider seriously the German approach, as long as priests as well as laymen would be involved. It is a most promising approach toward genuine understanding.

Catholics will have to revise some current notions of the world of religion if they would have themselves understood. Granted that the Catholic Church is the one Church founded by Christ himself and that it will prevail to the end of time, Catholics should not think that they can remain in their battlemented towers aloof from the non-Catholic world. Such a spirit is not even Christian. Catholics must know that Protestantism is not dying; that it is not overrun by secularism; and that because of the differences within it and some of the peculiar cults that spring out of it, it possesses no lasting convictions of sensible forms of belief. It numbers among its adherents not only countless numbers of holy, devout, sincere, and honest souls but countless numbers of men of good will who would gladly co-operate with Catholics in worth-while causes if given a chance. These people would think well of and trust Catholics much more fully if Catholics would be more willing to show them how and why. Bigotry there is, but not all actions taken by Protestants and Jews do have their origin in this unreasoning source. Catholics should always look to see in what actions of their own, in what misjudgments, in what imprudence, in what unwise power drives, this opposition has its source. But if genuine bigotry raises its head, there is no gain in answering bigotry with bigotry or aiming one's distrust at the whole non-Catholic world. The existence of bigotry and bias calls for more efforts at co-operation not less.

In the past religion was often the persecutor of men; today it is nonreligion. The forces of opposition to all religion possess power such as no religious leader of the ages gone by ever dreamed of. The forces of unbelief, however, are not confined to the countries where atheism is the official creed. They exist in the free lands and unfortunately are imbued with a cynical and hostile attitude toward all religious belief. Even in the free lands their hostility is cloaked in the garment of freedom and they would undermine religion and its institutions as useless relics of another age. But from the warring conditions within the religious forces comes the greatest support for the forces of unbelief. To the modern tyrant there is no difference between Jew and Gentile.

While dangers exist in institutionalizing interfaith discussions, there may be much to be said for the setting up of a National Commission on Interfaith Relations composed of well-qualified persons from the great faiths of America. The members would be chosen by representative groups of these faiths. It would be a continuing body and could draw in from time to time expert personnel. Such a commission could examine problems of day-to-day relationship among the religious groups and could provide for long-time study and discussion panels for the deeper problems of faith and morals. Its work, to be effective, would have to be carried on without publicity, except as it might deem it wise from time to time to issue a report on the results of its special studies. Representation of all three faiths would not be expected to take part in every discussion—for instance, certain problems could be profitably discussed only between Protestants and Catholics, others between Jews and Christians. In addition the commission could be on the alert for those temporary problems which could lead to great misunderstanding and hostility.

Not many years ago a group in France suggested a day of atonement to be observed by Catholics and Protestants with penitential prayers for the sins committed by one group against the other. In this lies a source of unity greater than any practical measures that could be considered. Nor is there any reason why it should not include Jews as well as Catholics and Protestants. In its observance, however, it should look to the future as well as the past, for there are temptations to the abuse of power in any group when it finds itself a large majority. To the prayers for the sins of the past might be added a prayer of humility and a solemn pledge for the future that never again will man's dignity or freedom be debased by religious persecution.

Why does a work on church and state devote so much space to interfaith relations? It would seem that all objections to the

Catholic Church in our country come down to this one problem —either as presented in the past or as demanding solution in the present. But is not this problem but part of a deeper and more far-reaching problem that we may sum up in the words distrust and fear? Does not the question of church and state relationship serve as the handy summary of many diverse questions? There are theories of church and state, but in the words of Grover Cleveland, is it not a condition rather than a theory that confronts us? Today men fear for the precious freedom that is theirs as never before. Forces seen and imagined trouble their days. As a supposed enemy of freedom the Catholic Church is feared. Do we not then, as Cardinal Lercaro suggests, need a new theology of freedom that will serve men in their present doubts and fears? Above all do we not need in this country a far greater degree of co-operation with non-Catholics—less parallel effort and more joint effort—in the tasks that confront us all?